KF
8748   Freund
.F678   On understanding
1977   the Supreme Court

DATE DUE

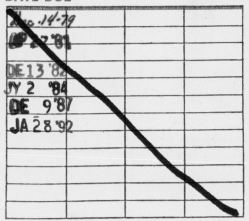

On Understanding
the Supreme Court

On Understanding the Supreme Court

A series of lectures delivered under the auspices of the Julius Rosenthal Foundation at Northwestern University School of Law, in April 1949

by

PAUL A. FREUND

PROFESSOR OF LAW, HARVARD UNIVERSITY

GREENWOOD PRESS, PUBLISHERS
WESTPORT, CONNECTICUT

Library of Congress Cataloging in Publication Data

Freund, Paul Abraham, 1908-
   On understanding the Supreme Court.

      Reprint of the 1949 ed. published by Little,
   Brown, Boston.
      CONTENTS: Concord and discord.--Portrait of a
   liberal judge: Mr. Justice Brandeis.--"Judge and
   Company" in constitutional law.
      1. United States. Supreme Court. I. North-
   western University, Evanston, Ill. Julius Rosenthal
   Foundation for General Law. II. Title.
   KF8748.F678 1977   347'.73'26   77-23550
   ISBN 0-8371-9699-X

Originally published in 1949 by Little, Brown and Company,
Boston

Reprinted with the permission of Northwestern University
and Professor Paul Freund

Reprinted in 1977 by Greenwood Press, Inc.

Library of Congress catalog card number   77-23550

ISBN 0-8371-9699-X

Printed in the United States of America

Foreword

The Julius Rosenthal Foundation for General Law

JULIUS ROSENTHAL, an eminent and beloved member of the Chicago bar, was born in Germany on September 17, 1828. He pursued his studies at the Universities of Heidelberg and Freiburg, came to Chicago in July, 1854, and was admitted to the bar in 1860. He was especially prominent as a practitioner in the law of wills and in probate and real estate law. As librarian of the Chicago Law Institute from 1867 to 1877 and again from 1888 to 1903, and as its president from 1878 to 1880, he was chiefly responsible for its development. He was a member of the First Board of State Law Examiners of Illinois, and its secretary from 1897 to 1899. He died May 14, 1905.

Julius Rosenthal was a lawyer of great learning and rare scholarly attainments. He labored long and earnestly to establish the highest standards of legal scholarship. Throughout his career, his interest in the Northwestern University School of Law was constantly manifested.

To honor his memory the Julius Rosenthal Foundation for General Law was established in 1919 by his son, Lessing Rosenthal, his daughter, Mrs. George Pick, and Charles H. Hamill, Max Hart, Harry Hart, Mark Cresap, Frank M. Peters, Leo P. Wormser, F. Howard Eldridge, Willard L. King, Magnus Myres, Mrs. Joseph Schaffner, and Mrs. Otto L. Schmidt, all of Chicago, and the Honorable Julian W. Mack, of New York. The income derived from the Foundation is, among other uses, applicable to the cultivation of legal literature, and particularly to the publication of meritorious essays, monographs, and books of a scientific or practical nature concerning the law; to the aid or encouragement of research in the field of legal literature and the preparation for publication of the results of such research; and to the delivery and publication of lectures on subjects concerning the law.

Preface

THIS VOLUME owes its origin to an invitation to deliver the Rosenthal Foundation lectures at the Law School of Northwestern University. More than customary courtesy impels this acknowledgment. For the invitation included a suggestion that the lectures be devoted to some aspects of the work of the Supreme Court, not excluding current controversies, and it was in response to that suggestion that the present text was prepared. It would not have been produced by spontaneous generation on the part of the author.

The Introduction and notes have been added to the lectures as delivered.

For memorable hospitality during the period when these lectures were given I am indebted to the law faculty of Northwestern, and particularly to Dean Harold Havighurst and Professors Brunson MacChesney and Nathaniel Nathanson, who served as a committee on arrangements.

P. A. F.

Cambridge, Massachusetts
July, 1949.

Contents

On Understanding
the Supreme Court

Introduction

IS THE LAW of the Supreme Court a reflection of the notions of "policy" held by its members? The question recalls the controversy over whether judges "make" or "find" the law. A generation or two ago it was thought rather daring to insist that judges make law. Old Jeremiah Smith, who began the teaching of law at Harvard after a career on the New Hampshire Supreme Court, properly deflated the issue. "Do judges make law?" he repeated. " 'Course they do. Made some myself." Of course Supreme Court Justices decide cases on the basis of their ideas of policy.

But to say this, as to say that judges make law, is not the end but only the beginning of sophistication. For there are levels of policy; and in Supreme Court litigation, values, like troubles, come not single file but in battalions. A case may present, in one aspect, an issue of civil liberties; it may also in-

volve issues of federalism, or of the relation of the
Court to the legislature, or of the standing of the
litigant to invoke judicial redress at all.

A topical catalog of decisions or of votes of individual Justices is likely perforce to focus on the win-
ning and losing litigants and the social interests
with which they are identified: big business, taxpayers, labor, political or religious minorities, and
so on. To rely on any such scheme of analysis is a
dubious approach to an understanding of the Supreme Court. To be sure, there have always been
occasions when all other policies or values or interests are submerged in a high tide of feeling on the
Court about a particular social cause. One such
occasion, which can be viewed with detachment
because three-quarters of a century have since
elapsed, was described by Mr. Justice Miller in his
correspondence. It concerned the prolific litigation
over state and municipal bonds issued often reck-
lessly in aid of private enterprises after the Civil
War. Writing to his brother-in-law, who had been
counsel in one of the controversies between bond-
holders and local taxpayers, Miller described the
judicial process in these cases:

I am sorry to see that you are so much disappointed at
the result of your case in our court. It is a result however

which I readily foresaw as soon as I discovered that it was a question of a demand growing out of a contract against a municipal corporation.

Our court or a majority of it are, if not monomaniacs, as much bigots and fanatics on that subject as is the most unhesitating Mahemodan in regard to his religion. In four cases out of five the case is decided when it is seen by the pleadings that it is a suit to enforce a contract against a city, or town, or a county. If there is a written instrument its validity is a foregone conclusion.[1]

However accurate Miller's description may have been, and however aptly it portrays certain workings of the Court in periods before and since, it will hardly be taken as a picture of the judicial function at its best. To set up similar preferences in contemporary causes as governing standards of performance for judges in our own day is scarcely a service to the administration of justice. Nor is it an adequate basis for an understanding of the work of the Supreme Court.

This little volume does not address itself, then, to tabular views on public questions of the day, but to certain questions which are believed to be relevant, at least, to an appreciation of the Supreme Court's tasks and decisions. Among the questions are these: How does the framework of democratic federal government within which the Court operates condition its activities? What are the hallmarks of a "liberal" Supreme Court Justice? What is the bearing of the strategy and tactics of counsel on the process of constitutional decision? In dramaturgical terms, the three chapters which follow may be said to deal, respectively, with plot, character, and supporting rôles. The first sketches some themes of concord and conflict. The second depicts some professional traits of a Justice who by common consent is entitled to be called "liberal." The third suggests the part played by the "company" in constitutional litigation.

The annotations do not go beyond April 1949, when the lectures were delivered. Whether late developments tend to confirm or to cloud any judgments herein expressed the reader will decide for himself. In any event, the purpose of the book is not so much to furnish judgments about the Court and its members as to indicate that because of the complexity of the Court's tasks such judgments are more difficult to reach than might be supposed, and to suggest inquiries relevant in reaching one's own.

I. Concord and Discord

TO UNDERSTAND the Supreme Court of the United States is a theme that forces lawyers to become philosophers. Alfred North Whitehead, suggesting that the key to a science of values will be found in aesthetics, remarked that the Supreme Court is seeking the aesthetic satisfaction of bringing the Constitution into harmony with the activities of modern America.[1] That is a satisfaction which the Court, in fits of anesthesia, has sometimes denied itself; but no more so than legislatures and executives, upon whom the pleasurable quest equally devolves.

If there is any philosophical problem that suggests its special counterpart in the task of the Court it is perhaps the problem of reconciling the One and the Many: one nation and many states; one Supreme Court and many organs of government; one Court speaking with many, often disconcertingly many, voices. In Great Britain, the Judicial Committee of the Privy Council always announces its decisions in a single opinion, for the decisions are in the form of advice to the Crown, and it is said that the Crown would be confused by conflicting advice. We attribute more hardihood to our bar, fortunately, than the British to their Crown.

The bar has not been entirely receptive to the compliment. Despite the reminder of Chief Justice Hughes that we ought not to expect much greater agreement on the difficult issues that come before the Court than we find in the higher realms of other intellectual disciplines — science, theology, philosophy [2] — we complain that the Many have obscured the One, that Whirl is King, having driven out Zeus. When invited to specify, the bar can draw on statistical tables of division in the present Court, catalogued and tabulated with all the deadly precision of a score sheet. It then appears that there are sharp cleavages in the Court in two major areas of decision: the field of civil liberties and the field of application of federal regulatory law. How significant is the discord, and what factors explain it? Unless we look behind the statistical compilations, in which votes are necessarily taken as values, we shall be in danger of emulating those institutes of social studies that my colleague T. R. Powell once described as places where the counters don't think and the thinkers don't count.

I shall consider first the field of civil liberties, or, as it is sometimes described, human rights contrasted with property rights. It is my conviction that the degree of concord in this area is much more important than the degree of discord, and that the themes of discord are not, if I may use the term, symmetrical.

The Court as a whole has given sanctuary to civil liberties that were not vindicated even by the Courts on which sat Holmes, Hughes, Brandeis, and Cardozo. The compulsory flag-salute in public schools, when challenged by a religious objector, was held not to present a substantial constitutional question by a Court which included Hughes and Brandeis. It has now been held, with Justices Roberts, Reed, and Frankfurter dissenting, to violate the Fourteenth Amendment.[3] The all-white primary, when established by rule of a party convention, was held in 1935 by a unanimous Court not to constitute state action in violation of the Fourteenth Amendment. The decision was overruled in 1944, with only Mr. Justice Roberts dissenting.[4] Restrictive covenants forbidding the sale of property to Negroes were until lately enforced in state courts, despite a claim of unconstitutional state action, with the acquiescence of a unanimous Court. Today, with the concurrence of all the Justices who participated in the consideration of the case, such enforcement is held a denial of equal protection of the laws.[5] In passing upon a city's requirement of a permit to speak in a public place, no one on the Court takes refuge in Holmes's early suggestion that because the city owns its parks and common it has a proprietor's right of exclusion.[6] In considering the ban on political activities of government employees, contained in the Hatch Act, the Court divided on the outcome, but no member found a complete solution in Holmes's aphorism that there may be a constitutional right to talk politics but not to be a policeman.[7]

Is the Court agreed that civil liberties are to be given a preferred position, that the criteria for deciding the validity of governmental action affecting "human rights" and "property rights" are different? Very recently Mr. Justice Frankfurter protested against the phrase "preferred position," particularly if it implied that under the First Amendment and the due-process clause of the Fourteenth there is a presumption of unconstitutionality attaching to any regulation of speech. He agreed, however, that a judge ought to be readier to find invasion of the Constitution where "free inquiry" is involved than in the "debatable area of economics." "Those liberties of the individual which history has attested as the indispensable conditions of an open as against a closed society," he said, "come to this Court with a momentum for respect lacking when appeal is made to liberties which derive merely from shifting economic arrangements." [8] In short, when freedom of the mind is imperiled by law, it is freedom that commands a momentum of respect; when property is imperiled, it is the lawmakers' judgment that commands respect. This dual standard may not precisely reverse the presumption of constitutionality in civil-liberties cases, but obviously it does set up a hierarchy of values within the due-process clause.

There is a remarkable core of agreement on the Court in this realm of values. It is remarkable because there has been no explicit agreement and little sustained discussion in the Court's opinions touching the basis for this scale of values — whether it is derived from the evidence of history regarding the relative social utility of different kinds of freedom, or is derived from convictions about the nature and duties of man, [9] or from an analysis of representative government.[10] It is the more remarkable because in applying the concept of liberty in the Fourteenth Amendment, the older Courts recognized liberty of contract before acknowledging liberty of speech as entitled to protection.[11] It is remarkable, finally, because other readings of history, other philosophical premises, and above all, other conceptions of the rôle of the Court can be found in our tradition.

The most impressive challenge to the double standard has come from Judge Learned Hand, in a memorial address on Chief Justice Stone. "Even before Justice Stone became Chief Justice," he said, "it began to seem as though, when 'personal rights' were in issue, something strangely akin to the discredited attitude towards the Bill of Rights of the old apostles of the institution of property, was regaining recognition. Just why property itself was not a 'personal right' nobody took the time to explain; and perhaps the inquiry would have been regarded as captious and invidious anyway; but the fact remained that in the name of the Bill of Rights the courts were upsetting statutes which were plainly compromises between conflicting interests, each of which had more than a merely plausible support in reason. That looked a good deal as though more specific directions could be found in the lapidary counsels of the Amendments than the successful school had been able to discover, so long as the dispute turned on property. It needed little acquaintance with the robust and loyal character of the Chief Justice to foretell that he would not be content with what to him was an opportunistic reversion at the expense of his conviction as to the powers of a court. He could not understand how the principle which he had all along supported, could mean that, when concerned with interests other than property, the courts should have a wider latitude for enforcing their own predilections, than when they were concerned with property itself." [12]

It is not uncommon that memorial addresses provide an even truer insight into the speaker than into the subject; and it is probably safer that the views so pointedly put by Judge Hand be ascribed to himself than to the late Chief Justice. At all events Judge Hand has contributed to clarity of analysis by reminding us that the relevant comparison is not between the enduring values of free inquiry and expression on the one hand, and transitory measures for the control of property on the other; the problem is harder than that. We are obliged to compare the ultimate values of property with those of free inquiry and expression, or to compare the legislative compromises in the two realms; for laws dealing with libel or sedition or sound trucks or a non-political civil service are as truly adjustments and accommodations as are laws fixing prices or making grants of monopolies.

Judge Hand's insistence on equality of values in constitutional decision can be matched by a persistent current of political thought. Indeed, the view that property itself is the matrix, the seed-bed, which must be conserved if other values are to flourish, has always had expression in American society. One need not revert to the middle ages, when, as Maitland observed, English constitutional law was a branch of the law of real property. Nor need one go to the modern philosophical Marxists to be told that personal liberties are but a reflection of the arrangements and pressures and powers in economic life. "Property must be secured," wrote John Adams, "or liberty cannot exist." [13] "The moment the idea is admitted into society," he warned, "that property is not as sacred as the laws of God, and that there is not a force of law and public justice to protect it, anarchy and tyranny commence." [14] And Adams's great antagonist, John Taylor of Caroline County, Virginia, was just as emphatic: "Is not

a power of transferring property by pensions, boun-
ties, corporations and exclusive privileges; and even
of bestowing publick money by the unlimited will
of legislative bodies, as dangerous to liberty, as a
power of doing the same thing by the instrumental-
ity of a privileged church? Is the casuistry consist-
ent, which denies to a government the power of
infringing the freedom of religion, and yet invests it
with a despotism over the freedom of property? . . .
Blackstone has treated of 'the rights of persons, and
the rights of things;' but the rights of man include
life, liberty and property, according to the prevalent
fashion of thinking in the United States. The last
right is the chief hinge upon which social happiness
depends. It is therefore extremely important to as-
certain, whether it is secured by the same principle
with our other rights." Thus John Taylor, the philos-
opher of agrarian democracy.[15] The debates on suffrage in the 1820's produced some frank and searching inquiries into the rôle of property. Daniel
Webster in Massachusetts and James Kent in New
York made statements which have become classic.
Said Webster: "Life and personal liberty are, no
doubt, to be protected by law; but property is also
to be protected by law, and is the fund out of which
the means for protecting life and liberty are usually

furnished. We have no experience that teaches us,
that any other rights are safe, where property is not
safe." [16] And Kent, looking about him, was lugubri-
ous, as are the Kents of every age: "My opinion is
that the admission of universal suffrage and a licen-
tious press are incompatible with government and
security to property, and that the government and
character of this country are going to ruin." [17]

Property, indeed, came to have a religious sanction in the evangelism of the gilded age. In 1868,
that *annus mirabilis* which gave us at once the Fourteenth Amendment and Cooley's *Constitutional
Limitations*, President Hopkins of Williams College
published *The Law of Love and Love as Law*. "The
Right to Property," he wrote, "reveals itself through
an original desire. . . . Without this society could
not exist. . . . It will be found too, historically, that
the general well-being and progress of society has
been in proportion to the freedom of every man to
gain property in all legitimate ways, and to security
in its possession. . . . The acquisition of property is
required by love, because it is a powerful means of
benefiting others." [18] Latterly the new humanism has
insisted on the centrality of property in civilization.
Paul Elmer More, in his essay on Property and Law,
advanced this philosophy of history: "Although,

probably, the rude government of barbarous chiefs, when life was precarious and property unimportant, may have dealt principally with wrongs to person, yet the main care of advancing civilization has been for property. After all, life is a very primitive thing. Nearly all that makes it more significant to us than to the beast is associated with our possessions — with property, all the way from the food we share with the beasts, to the most refined products of the human imagination. To the civilized man *the rights of property are more important than the right to life.*" [19]

Of course these encomia on property have as many meanings as they have motivations. But for all its ambiguities, a concept of property in some form was elevated to first rank by a long line of American figures both influential and unabashed. This strain of thought finds no hospitality on the Court today. To that extent the Justices can share the proud solace of the German artist who exclaimed, "If I am nothing else, at least I am a contemporary!" Certainly it is not discreditable in a judge, even a judge interpreting the Constitution, to be a contemporary. Vistas grow, perspectives lengthen, reflection deepens, and new meanings come to seem fitting for such projecting terms as "liberty" or "due process of law," and "establishment of religion" or "the free exercise thereof." The judge need only be careful not to confuse a climate of opinion with the heat of the day, not to mistake the gusts of a local storm for the steady winds of doctrine. Is not this the answer to be made for judges to the question of the troubled poet who describes a clump of windswept trees and asks:

Is it as plainly in our living shown
By bend and twist, which way the wind hath blown?

Of late, it must be confessed, the new liberty has grown to such a flourishing estate that at times it seems to embrace a new property in the guise of freedom of speech and assembly. The transformation of economic pressures into rights of free expression has been partially accomplished in labor controversies. Picketing is indeed a hybrid, comprising elements of persuasion, information, and publicity together with elements of non-verbal conduct, economic pressure and signals for action. It is scarcely surprising that judgments on the Court should differ on the weight to be accorded these elements in fixing the point at which picketing becomes subject to the state's intervention and control.

There are, however, limits beyond which the new

property in the position of organized labor will not be carried. The test came early in 1949. Does labor have a right of association so fundamental that the Constitution draws a line of fire around the power of the union to exclude non-members from employment? Are agreements for a closed shop constitutionally immune from the authority of government to regulate or prohibit them? Some observers were inclined to believe that on this issue the Court would be sorely rent. And yet with the concurrence of all the Justices who participated in the case the Court has now sustained the authority of the state to prohibit closed-shop agreements, at least where the state also prohibits interference by employers with the organization of labor.[20] The position of the union toward the parasitic non-joiner is no more sacrosanct than the position of the employer toward the union members.

The Court is doubtless as aware as the rest of us that the effective enjoyment of civil liberties requires a degree of command over material resources, just as the exercise of virtue posits the practical capacity to choose one satisfaction and reject another. As Professor Hocking has judiciously put it: "To contemporary consciousness it has become an axiom that there can be *no freedom without provision;* for

a large part of mankind the main task of freedom is at the economic level; and business, as Beardsley Ruml has shown, has to share this task with politics. But it remains true that provision, work, and leisure are not enough; the most abundant provision is not human freedom unless a man remains the unhampered director of his powers of thought and action. Concrete freedom requires both factors." [21] The difficulty of translating this into constitutional terms is the dangerous impropriety of committing to the Court the task of defining minimum standards of material provision.

And so the Court has left to the forum of public opinion the major issue of our time, how far economic community is essential to human freedom. The Constitution enforces no answer, equal protection of the laws in its narrow sense apart, though the question is an old one for the makers of constitutions. On May 1, 1949, we will have celebrated (or we should) the three hundredth anniversary of that remarkable product of the Puritan Revolution and its army, *An Agreement of the Free People of England.* This seminal document, the final version of the platform of the Leveller group, foreshadowed universal manhood suffrage, religious toleration, the abolition of imprisonment for debt, and other of our modern guarantees; but it also provided that "it shall not be in the power of any Representative, in any wise, to . . . level men's estates, destroy Propriety, or make all things Common. . . ." [22] If we take pride in the modernity of the authors of this document, Lilburne, Walwyn, Prince, and Overton, we may also take counsel at the modernity of their treatment; for they were denounced with the hateful and quite unmerited epithet of the day, "Levellers"; and the document itself was drafted in the cells of the Tower of London.

The Levellers were answered by the left wing of the Puritan reformers, whose symbol was their digging in St. George's Hill to convert it into a collective farm. In 1652 appeared the Diggers' *Law of Freedom in a Platform,* which analyzed the essentials of liberty: "Some say, It [Freedom] lies in the free use of Trading, and to have Patents, Licenses, and Restraints removed: But this is a Freedom under the Will of a Conqueror. Others say, It is true Freedom to have Ministers to preach, and for people to hear whom they will, without being restrained or compelled from or to any form of worship: But this is an unsettled Freedom. . . . True Commonwealths Freedom lies in the Free Enjoyment of the Earth." [23]

Our Constitution and our judges have left our St.

George's Hills to be acquired or not as the legislature may decide; if one is acquired as a common it may have to be opened to the speeches of Diggers of all persuasions, though not to their implements of labor. This is the dominant harmony within the Court today.

There are of course themes of discord in the score of the present Court. But just as it would be idle to close our ears to these themes so it would be a distortion to hear them as a single discord. There are at least three distinct lines of conflict, it seems to me, in the area of civil liberties.

The first lies in the relative regard which is given to what may be called aggressive and passive liberties. On the whole the active proselyting interests have been given greater sanctuary than the quiet virtues or the right of privacy. The emergence of the militant sect of Jehovah's Witnesses has dramatized this conflict. A fairly stable majority of one has shielded the Witnesses from non-discriminatory taxes on their distribution of literature, from local ordinances forbidding the ringing of doorbells by solicitors, and from regulations requiring permits for the use of sound trucks.[24] The Court here has acted virtually as a legislative drafting bureau for municipal authorities. The zeal of Jehovah's Witnesses can be kept within bounds by properly framed regulations. Notice posted by the householder himself that he does not wish to be disturbed may be made the basis for criminal prosecution if the notice is disregarded. And sound trucks can presumably be regulated in the matter of decibels and the hours of their use. While in the control of economic activities a government may extend its regulatory hand beyond the strict necessities of the problem, at least as those necessities might appear to a judge, the control of evangelism must be virtually the least possible control needed to achieve the result. The states are almost in the legal position of the individual who may act in self-defense if he uses no more force than necessary.

While the privilege of righteous peaceful aggression has thus been sanctified, the privilege of private belief and of security from intrusion has been profaned. A religious objector to war is unable by reason of his belief to become a member of the bar in Illinois, and the Supreme Court approves because he cannot conscientiously subscribe to the state constitution, which authorizes the calling out of militia, even though it has been traditional in practice to exempt genuinely conscientious objectors and even though the state reserves the power to punish disobedience in an actual emergency.[25] Moreover, the immunity from unreasonable search and seizure has had only wavering protection. It is worth more than passing note that the rather stable majority in the cases of aggressive liberties tends to dissolve when freedom from search and seizure is challenged, so that it falls to the lot of a differently constituted group to vindicate most powerfully this liberty, which can fairly be deemed basic to many others.[26] For in a police state there can be few if any liberties more obnoxious and indeed impossible than the liberty to record and transmit one's thoughts and one's transactions without fear of the unchecked official eavesdropper.

In sum, there are civil liberties which point to insurgency and there are those which look to integrity. Whether by reason of temperament or experience or the variant readings of history, different judges have found in these realms different constitutional accommodations between liberty and authority.

The second theme of discord turns on the clear-and-present-danger test. One group on the Court finds in this criterion a standard for judging most limitations on human expression; others believe that the test is frequently inapt. The conflict is exemplified when the test is used to mark the province of speech uttered about a judge or about a case before him. Does the Constitution render the publication of threatening language immune from punishment as contempt of court unless there is a clear and present danger that the judgment of the judge will be distorted and the even-handed administration of justice corrupted? Or is the temperate and undisturbed administration of justice itself so fundamental a value in the safeguarding of civil liberties that speech may be punished which is calculated to deflect the judicial judgment even though there is no showing that in the particular instance deflection was a clear and present danger?

The clear-and-present-danger test had its origin, of course, with Mr. Justice Holmes in sedition cases. It is apparent that he found in the test a useful measure of the range of free discussion where our institutions are challenged in the public forum. The test is pretty clearly drawn from the criminal law, and in particular from Holmes's analysis of the criminal law as scholar and state court judge; [27] for the criminal law is necessarily concerned with the line at which innocent preparation ends and a guilty conspiracy or attempt begins. These standards of proximity and degree as Holmes called them were made to do service in constitutional law in marking the line between innocent talk and guilty incitement to action. The state may not punish open talk, however hateful; not for the hypocritical reason that Hyde Parks are a safety-valve, but because a bit of sense may be salvaged from the odious by minds striving to be rational, and this precious bit will enter into the amalgam which we forge. At least that is our faith, and if we are reminded that the irrational element furnishes the more powerful charge in the process of transmutation, we may answer that we dare not concentrate the whole enterprise in a few censors whose pathology may be even more fatal.

But the test is founded on the importance of persuasion by unfettered and contentious talk in an open forum. It would not be applied today to protect a voluble atheist during services in a church. It was not applied in Holmes's day to statements made out of court in an effort to sway a magistrate whose office is meant to insulate him from precisely such pressures. It is hardly surprising that those judges on the Court who value relatively highly what I have called the quiet virtues are the judges who have insisted that the integrity of the judicial function may be safeguarded by law without a showing of clear and present danger.[28]

The lines of division were broken down again in passing on the validity of the Hatch Act. In that Act Congress had weighed more highly the value of a disinterested public service than the value of full political activity by government employees. The relevant provisions of the Act were sustained, and some of the judges who insisted upon the clear-and-present-danger test as applied to contempt of court were nevertheless willing to appraise these restrictions on political activity of civil servants without inquiring whether such activity put public administration definitely and imminently in jeopardy.[29]

The truth is that the clear-and-present-danger test is an oversimplified judgment unless it takes account also of a number of other factors: the relative seriousness of the danger in comparison with the value of the occasion for speech or political activity; the availability of more moderate controls than those which the state has imposed; and perhaps the specific intent with which the speech or activity is launched. No matter how rapidly we utter the phrase "clear and present danger," or how closely we hyphenate the words, they are not a substitute for the weighing of values. They tend to convey a delusion of certitude when what is most certain is the complexity of the strands in the web of freedoms which the judge must disentangle.

A third issue dividing the Court is the relevance of federalism in the vindication of civil liberties. In enforcing civilized standards of criminal procedure the Court as a whole has found greater warrant for intervention in cases of federal than of state convictions. The now celebrated *McNabb* rule,[30] excluding from evidence confessions obtained while the prisoner is held by federal authorities without prompt arraignment, has no counterpart in cases from the state courts, where some element of actual coercion must be shown in order to exclude a confession.[31] The *McNabb* case is a judge-made rule of evidence enforcing a federal legislative rule of arraignment. Mr. Justice Frankfurter wrote the opinion with only Mr. Justice Reed dissenting. In these cases of criminal procedure it is not uncommon to find this alignment but with a shifting majority, while in picketing cases their rôles in finding immunity are reversed. It was Mr. Justice Reed who wrote the Court's opinion and Mr. Justice Frankfurter who dissented in the tragic case of *Fisher* v. *United States*,[32] sustaining the death sentence imposed on a semi-literate Negro for a killing which

the jury might well have found was unpremeditated
had the trial judge guided the jury with the psychological perception shown in the dissenting opinion in the Supreme Court. Mr. Justice Frankfurter
has recently given voice to his impatience with the
Court's readiness to review state decisions at the
behest of those who excite our sympathies, where
the state procedures were not properly observed in
pressing the claim of unfairness. The Court is not,
he said bluntly, a super-legal-aid bureau.[33] And yet
in cases like Fisher's, arising in a lower federal court,
no one has been readier than he to employ the super-
visory power of the Court to enforce meticulously
fair standards in criminal trials. Likewise, on the
side of substantive federal criminal law, he has been
particularly sensitive, along with Justices Murphy,
Jackson, and Rutledge, to the abuses that inhere in
the facile use of conspiracy charges as a means of
cumulating sentences and of making all too complex the procedural task of individual defendants.[34]

The problem of the standards governing the states
has now been enmeshed in the controversy over the
issue whether the Fourteenth Amendment embodies
the entire national Bill of Rights. Mr. Justice Black
has fought valiantly to establish this proposition
notwithstanding over half a century of adjudication

to the contrary. Indeed this effort, buttressed with great historical research in the *Adamson* case,[35] appears to be the culmination of a persistent search by Mr. Justice Black for a textual basis on which to predicate the maximum protection of civil liberties with a modicum of protection for interests of property. Other members of the Court have employed a double standard for interests of personality and property on philosophic grounds, but Mr. Justice Black is understandably apprehensive that such a measure of values may be fleeting over a period of time. He would therefore reject standards for which he reserves that most opprobrious epithet "natural law," [36] in favor of the compulsion of the constitutional words themselves, if in the light of language and history they can bear his reading.

Early in his justiceship he advanced the view that the "persons" protected by the due process clause of the Fourteenth Amendment are natural persons and not corporations.[37] But how were the civil liberties of natural persons to be safeguarded under the protection of "life, liberty and property" in the due-process clause unless the economic interests of such persons were to claim parallel treatment? A tentative answer seems to have been ventured in *Hague* v. *CIO*. Although the right of assembly and freedom of speech were upheld by a majority of the Court, in a separate opinion Justices Roberts and Black united in placing the result on the "privileges and immunities of citizens of the United States" rather than the due-process clause.[38] Mr. Justice Black was apparently reconciled to the conclusion that such protection under the privileges and immunities clause would be limited to citizens of the United States, excluding aliens as well as corporations; but at the same time the clause might be interpreted to include the civil liberties enumerated in the first eight Amendments without extending the same cloak of protection to economic interests under the due-process clause; that clause would presumably be left as a guarantee simply of procedural justice.

This revival of the privileges and immunities clause was put to the test in reviewing the contempt convictions of Harry Bridges and the *Los Angeles Times*. A case could hardly have been more fiendishly conceived for the purpose of testing the source of the guarantee of freedom of speech and press, since the petitioners were respectively an alien and a corporation. The Court in an opinion by Mr. Justice Black found it possible to reverse the conviction on Fourteenth Amendment grounds; but without specifically replying to the pointed inquiry of the dis-

senters who asked to be informed just what clause of
the Fourteenth Amendment was being invoked.[39]
Finally in the *Adamson* case the inquiry was met by
the assertion in the dissent of Mr. Justice Black that
the provisions of the first section of the Fourteenth
Amendment, taken "separately, and as a whole" in-
corporate the national Bill of Rights.[40] This position,
which has not commended itself to a majority of the
Court, would achieve to the utmost the objectives
suggested a little earlier: a guarantee of civil liberties
to all individuals, citizens and aliens; a residue of
procedural guarantees in the vague and inclusive
due-process clause; and the relegation of substantive
economic interests to the discard of "natural law."

But it is one thing to slam the door of the due-
process clause, and another to keep it shut. Of the
four Justices who joined in the *Adamson* dissent,
two — Justices Murphy and Rutledge — were explicit in serving notice that the Bill of Rights provides content, but only a minimum content, for the
Fourteenth Amendment. Abuses may be unconstitutional though not specifically enumerated and described. And even Justices Black and Douglas, the
other two members of the group, are not content, as
Professor John Frank has acutely observed, to rest
on the specific guarantees of the first eight Amend-

ments. For they are no less persuaded than their brethren that, for example, criminal statutes may be unconstitutional when they are too vague and indefinite to form a guide to conduct, although there is nothing in the text of the Bill of Rights which denounces laws on that score, save as the standard may be smuggled into the due-process clause.[41] One man's natural law may turn out to be simply another's fighting verities. A righteous repudiation of natural law is apt to recall T. H. Huxley's renunciation of rhetoric: "Let me observe, in passing, that rhetorical ornament is not in my way, and that gilding refined gold would, to my mind, be less objectionable than varnishing the fair face of truth with that pestilent cosmetic, rhetoric." [42]

The whole episode of the debate on the general meaning of the Fourteenth Amendment is unfortunate. The controversy magnifies differences and obscures agreements. The Court is agreed that the Amendment protects aliens and corporations (at least when they conduct the newspaper business). The Court as a whole is hardly concerned with the question whether the Seventh Amendment's guarantee of a petit jury in civil cases involving more than twenty dollars shall be made applicable to the states by the Fourteenth. On the issue of unlawful search and seizure some members of the Court are evidently ready to give greater protection in the name of basic civilized standards than would be given by others in reliance on the specific guarantee.

Moreover, as a controversy over the meaning of history the debate on the Fourteenth Amendment can hardly be resolved. Whatever the general language of the sponsors of the Amendment, they did not squarely address themselves to the question whether each and every enumerated right in the first eight Amendments was meant to be carried into the Fourteenth; and much less can we find an answer in the views of the legislators who ratified in the states. Besides, the states have adapted their procedures on the assumption that there was room for experimentation, particularly in the substitution of other forms for the grand jury. And the guarantee against self-incrimination hardly demands slavish adoption by the states of all the peripheral rules which have grown up around the practice in the federal courts, so long as confessions obtained by coercing the will are ruled out, as they are, under the due-process clause.

The pressing issue centers on the right of indigent defendants in criminal cases to have counsel appointed as a matter of course. In the federal courts this has been required since 1938 on the ground that it is commanded by the Sixth Amendment.[43] A majority of the Court has been unwilling to apply this blanket rule to state prosecutions, preferring a case-by-case review looking to the essential fairness or unfairness of the procedure.[44] One may hope that a majority of the Court will turn to the view that the appointment of counsel is as indispensable to the just and even-handed administration of the criminal law in the state courts as in the federal courts. They would be helped to reach this conclusion by avowing frankly that the Sixth Amendment does not furnish the real reason for the requirement in the federal courts. It seems more nearly true to regard that Amendment as having simply conferred the right on the accused to employ counsel — a right which of course was by no means assured prior to the adoption of the Constitution. If the right to have counsel appointed in the federal courts is acknowledged to rest on a pervasive sense of justice it should be extended to state prosecutions as an element of due process of law. This would be a happy *dénouement* of the dramatic, the over-dramatic, clash over the Fourteenth Amendment which has drawn so heavily on the energies of the Court.

These cleavages in the Court — on aggressive and

passive liberties, on the clear-and-present-danger test, and on the relevance of federalism — hardly constitute a Great Divide. Intensity of feeling, however, generally varies inversely with the distance separating the disputants, as more obloquy has usually been heaped on heretics than on infidels.

It is not remarkable that the process of constitutional decision has become more self-conscious, more avowedly an expression of political philosophy, than ever before. Our present judges have gone to school, as it were, to Holmes and Cardozo. And they are as aware as the rest of us that clichés are paperweight weapons in a world of colliding civilizations. What is perhaps more remarkable is that the process of statutory construction has likewise become an aspect of political philosophy.

The familiar canons and maxims of interpretation, if not paper-thin, are at all events wooden. Not even Maitland's compression of the canons to five jocular words in describing his practice as a member of the Council of the Senate of Cambridge University is a wholly reliable guide: "I always stretch a statute"[45] — though some would no doubt insist that it explains as well as anything else the current practice of the Court.

The treatment of statutes is a philosophical exercise because it is another aspect of the Many and the One — one state, many organs, of which the judiciary is one. A recurring pattern of conflict will describe the judge's problem: How far is a court free to reconsider an earlier doubtful decision when the legislature meanwhile has not acted to change the law? The question is thrust on the Court in many manifestations. Does the Sherman Act now encompass insurance contracts, though the making of them was assumed in 1890 not to be interstate commerce and the Act has not been amended? [46] Does an income tax expressly laid on dividends to the extent permitted by the Sixteenth Amendment authorize a tax on all stock dividends when at the time of the statute only a limited class had been held constitutionally taxable? [47] Does the Naturalization Act, repeating earlier language requiring the applicant to support and defend the Constitution and laws of the United States against all enemies, foreign and domestic, authorize an oath to bear arms to be exacted of a conscientious objector, when the earlier law had been so construed by a divided Court? [48] Does the Mann Act apply to polygamy, when the Court had held it to include non-commercial vice? [49] Each of the earlier decisions had been roundly criticized.

Should a judge's impulse toward self-correction be checked because of apparent acquiescence by Congress in the original sin? The answer should depend on a closer examination of the legislature's inaction in the particular case, and on the viability of an overruling decision. It is not so important how these questions are answered as it is that they be asked.

I have heard it said that the courts should always leave the function of correction to the legislature; that as this is in the legislature's power it is the legislature's business. But surely this is a gross overstatement. The legislature's inaction may reflect satisfaction with the fluidity of the judicial process rather than with the particular precedent. The legislature may be reluctant to pose a constitutional issue too sharply, as where it prefers not to make general statutory language explicitly retroactive, or where it retains broad constitutional terms in a statute without specific amendment. To defer to the legislature in these circumstances would be playing an Alphonse-Gaston game.

I have also heard it suggested, at the other extreme, that the courts should wholly disregard legislative inaction, for self-correction is the proper business of judges, and we are meant to be ruled by the directions of the old legislature as judges from time to time fathom those directions, until the living legislature acts positively with all the proper formalities. But at the very least the inaction of Congress in the face of strong pressure to change the law may well lead judges to consider whether their decision was as egregiously wrong as they might otherwise suppose. Moreover, action and inaction are only convenient terms of degree. A specific vote rejecting an amendment to the law is, I suppose, positive and formal action, though even this may be explained away on the evidence as a choice to leave the matter open-ended for the courts. Short of such a specific vote, there may be a reconsideration of the larger legislative problem, eventuating in a new Act without any formal statutory reference to the point of the Court's decision. This nevertheless provides a new starting point, a pointer held in living hands, and the silence of the statute on the precise issue becomes relevant and must be interpreted by some such analysis of internal evidence as I have suggested.

Some members of the Court are more sensitive to the legislative silences than others. They are more sensitive, too, to what I have called the problem of the viability of an overruling decision. Will it leave in its wake so great a wreckage that the business is best left to the legislature, which can act prospectively or can make the needed adjustments to remove inequities? Mr. Justice Douglas in the stock-dividend case said that such considerations are "none of our business." [50] But when judgment is poised, the consequences can scarcely be disregarded as part of judicial statecraft. It is significant that on a number of recent occasions counsel for the government, recognizing the dislocations that would result from the advanced position which they were urging on the Court, took pains to assert that they had obtained informal assurances from administrative or legislative leaders that remedial regulations or legislation would be sponsored to take care of inequities. It is even more significant that on each occasion this argument was thrown back at its proponents by a segment of the Court, particularly Justices Jackson and Frankfurter, who retorted that the whole matter should be left to Congress if the shattering of precedent by the Court would leave debris which Congress would have to clear away. [51]

The consequences to be expected from an overruling decision are relevant, but the inability or unwillingness of Congress or the executive to deal with them may at times have been exaggerated. In

1938 the Court abandoned the doctrine of immunity of salaries of state employees from federal taxation.[52] The government had not argued for so sweeping a decision; the taxing statute and the regulations were couched in the most general terms; it was not until the case was pending that the regulations were changed, and then only to include public salaries unless constitutionally immune from taxation; finally, a month before the decision the President felt it advisable to ask Congress for specific legislation, taxing state salaries and waiving immunity of federal salaries from state taxation, declaring, "The Federal Government does not now levy income taxes on the hundreds of thousands of State, county, and municipal employees." [53] Despite this concatenation of cautions the Court made a new law. The taxpayer, asking a rehearing, urged that the decision be applied prospectively only, to avoid injustices. Solicitor General Jackson agreed that the Court had power thus to limit its decision but maintained that the problem of caring for inequities should be left to the resourcefulness of administrative regulations and action by Congress.[54] In fact, Congress responded to the problem by enacting the Public Salaries Act of 1939, making the federal tax prospective only, and waiving federal immunity on a similar basis.[55] I suggest that there was wisdom as well as advocacy in the Solicitor General's position.

The implication to be drawn from divisions on these issues is not that those who are laggard in reinterpreting statutes are less hospitable than their brethren to the claims of collectors of internal revenue, or more hostile to the claims of conscientious objectors, or more opposed to controls over restraints of trade. The implication is rather that some members of the Court rebel more sharply at what they conceive to be an effort to push them farther along the road to Utopia than the elected lawmakers have been propelled. In erecting what Judge Learned Hand has aptly called a bias against bias,[56] they may have allowed themselves to be repelled too strongly away from their private bent and the advances of their brethren. If anything more is needed to assure a disinterested judgment than a bias against bias, it is perhaps a bias against bias against bias. For balance may be lost by leaning backwards as well as forwards.

How can the professional, or indeed the lay, observer of the Court's work better understand the concord and discord that he finds? He can recognize that because of the Court's special position in relation to our political as well as social institutions, it perforce operates in more than one realm of values; and that to assess those values requires judicial art, not artfulness. He can strive to understand the pressures of advocacy and of personal preference and the defensive mechanism which these evoke in the judicial mind. He can endeavor to appreciate the complexities of judging before criticizing the simplicities of voting. He can refrain from assigning judges to appointed places in a heavenly choir, to tiers in a celestial hierarchy. By doing these things we can perhaps give point to the story of the Irish cleric who was asked by a parishioner what the difference was between the cherubim and seraphim, and who answered, "I think that there was once a difference between them, but they have made it up."

II. Portrait of a Liberal Judge: Mr. Justice Brandeis

THE APPOINTMENT of a lawyer to the Supreme Court naturally tempts us to inquire into his earlier career, and particularly the economic interests he represented, for a clue to his future performance as a judge. What is past is prologue, to be sure; but the drama as it unfolds may be full of surprise. A crude economic interpretation of the judicial office ignores too many elements of character. The taking of the robe, an experience at once emancipating and humbling, is apt to dissolve old ties and to quicken the sense that there is no escape from that judgment of one's successors which is called history.

The record of the Court supplies many cautions against the generalization that the lawyer is father to the judge. It was a successful lawyer for shipping interests, Henry Billings Brown, who as Mr. Justice

Brown delivered a memorable dissent in the income-tax cases: " . . . the decision involves nothing less than a surrender of the taxing power to the moneyed class. . . . I hope it may not prove the first step toward the submergence of the liberties of the people in a sordid despotism of wealth." [1] It was a successful railroad lawyer, Stanley Matthews, once rejected by the Senate because of his clientele, who as Mr. Justice Matthews expressed what is perhaps the most salient proposition of constitutional law next to Marshall's "we must never forget, that it is *a constitution* we are expounding." Mr. Justice Matthews, in resisting a request that an Act of Congress be declared unconstitutional, declared that the Court "has no jurisdiction to pronounce any statute, either of a State or of the United States, void, because irreconcilable with the Constitution, except as it is called upon to adjudge the legal rights of litigants in actual controversies. In the exercise of that jurisdiction, it is bound by two rules, to which it has rigidly adhered, one, never to anticipate a question of constitutional law in advance of the necessity of deciding it; the other never to formulate a rule of constitutional law broader than is required by the precise facts to which it is to be applied. These rules are safe guides to sound judgment. It is the dictate of

wisdom to follow them closely and carefully." [2] It
was another railroad lawyer, Joseph P. Bradley, who
as Mr. Justice Bradley protested against the use of
the due-process clause to review the regulation of
railroad rates by the states, and who would have
permitted the states to regulate interstate rates until
Congress assumed the responsibility. [3] And it was
Harlan F. Stone, whose record in sustaining the
validity of social legislation needs no comment, who
had written in 1916 by way of commentary on Her-
bert Spencer's "The Sins of Legislators" that "Spencer's vigorous warning furnishes food for thought
and will perhaps inspire with caution the zealous
advocates of such sweeping legislative changes as
are involved in the many proposals for the various
types of pension law, and minimum wage statutes,
and modern legislation of similar character." [4] The
list could be extended.

The instances I have given exemplify the successful caretaker of powerful groups becoming the disinterested judge. What of the lawyer who has been
identified with quite different professional interests
— representation of the consumer or the poorly organized, or service in the cause of law reform? For
him as a judge what are the hallmarks of liberalism?
Shall his judgeship be a continuance or indeed an

intensification of his earlier concerns; or for him too is there a problem of adjustment to his new rôle, a change of pace or of direction?

I know of no better approach to this question than through the experience of Mr. Justice Brandeis. A coldly passionate and relentless adversary, he had and he showed little of the conventional respect for the captains and the kings and the mandarins in our society, while he had a fervid regard for the potentialities of the obscure. Such a man, so irreverent toward the god of things as they are, would be a clear and present danger on the bench; so at least it was thought by many.

They overlooked a number of significant factors in his social thought as a citizen and counsellor at law. For one thing he was a devoted friend of private capitalism, so long as he could define what was the essence of capitalism and what its excrescences. In addition, his enormous driving force was controlled by an equally remarkable sense of balance. If he was a devil on wheels to his opponents, he was the austere judge to his clients. The rôle of "counsel for the situation" appealed to his constructive talents and to his faith in the power of reasoned thought to find accommodations within the framework of principle. After guiding an association of employers to victory against a striking union, he converted the congratulatory meeting into a forum for a lecture to his clients on the just claims of labor, which included a greater share in the responsibilities of industrial management. In similar vein, when addressing a gathering of labor leaders he was quick to seize the occasion as an opportunity to win their support for the unpopular cause of scientific management.[5]

But when every allowance is made for these tempering attributes, it is true that for Brandeis no less than for other judges the transition from private citizen to Supreme Court judge posed some basic issues. Many of his most deep-seated convictions were at odds not only with prevailing judicial conceptions but with the assumptions of legislators who could fairly be called progressive. What was there in the career of Brandeis as a Justice that marked him as a liberal?

I suggest that his liberalism did not consist in a preponderance of votes (if such indeed was the record) for the government or against large corporations. I suggest that his liberalism as a judge lay rather in an essential morality of mind, and that this quality is his essential and enduring contribution to the work of the Court. What I call his morality of mind gives a coherence to his labors that transcends his contribution to this or that particular sector of the law, impressive as those contributions have been.

I would suggest four principal manifestations of the essential quality of mind which he brought to his task: (1) an insistence on knowledge as indispensable to judging; (2) rejection of opportunism; (3) an insistence on jurisdictional and procedural observances; and (4) rejection of sentimentality.

(1) In his own phrase, knowledge must precede understanding and understanding should precede judging.[6] If any *vade mecum* was inscribed on the tablets of his mind I surmise that it would have been these words. They explain a good deal about his methods that might otherwise appear singular and unrelated. His belief in the primacy of facts was apparent even in the process of preparing an opinion. However much he encouraged his law clerks to present the results of their legal research in a form which might be directly useful in drafting an opinion, he took on himself the burden of drafting the statement of facts. This was his private assurance that he would not be seduced by the fascination of legal analysis until he had grounded himself in the realities of the case as they were captured in the record.

It was essentially the same sense of the controlling vitality of facts that produced the so-called Brandeis brief at the bar and its counterpart in his richly documented opinions on the bench. No one attached more weight than he to the presumption of constitutionality attaching to acts of the legislature; and yet he was rarely content to rest his judgment there without the confirmation which he found in a study of the context of legislation. In his opinions the technique of the Brandeis brief was generally employed to sustain the legislative judgment. But on occasion the same technique, reflecting the same insatiable passion to know, was employed to suggest that what had once been constitutional might be questionable in the light of facts that had markedly changed. A remand of the cause for further findings was for him an important and valuable procedural mechanism. He employed it, for example, when he raised the question whether to place the cost of grade-crossing removal on a railroad might have become constitutionally less tolerable with the great increase in competitive traffic on the highways.[7]

This readiness to see significance in a fuller exhibit of facts, whatever the direction in which the facts might point, suggests the next aspect of the morality of his mind, namely his rejection of opportunism.

(2) It is hardly likely that anyone came to the Supreme Court with a more closely articulated set of convictions than those which Brandeis held. His views on the most specific and particular issues could be readily predicted by one who was familiar with the basic premises of his thinking. Inexorable as were the implications of these premises, they were not congenial, as I have said, to much that passed current in the world of social thought. He believed that capitalism succeeded only as it provided larger and larger opportunities for the sharing of responsibility, and that it was corrupted as power became more and more divorced from those who were its subjects. As economic controls have become more anonymous and remote, it is a commonplace that the state has felt obliged to intervene in order to mitigate the cruelties which are the residual deposit of the machine. Brandeis took a fundamentally different approach to the rôle of the state, conceiving it to be primarily an instrument whereby incentives are provided for the responsible and socially useful exercise of power. Hence his sovereign measure was the discouragement of bigness through a graduated tax on gross assets. Hence

too, in his conception of social security, he had a strong preference for the Wisconsin or company-reserve plan of unemployment insurance over the state-wide pooled fund; for the Wisconsin plan was meant as an incentive to each employer to regularize his employment, while the competing plan was designed as a palliative for what was accepted as the inevitable and impersonal doom of unemployment under conditions of capitalism. It is no secret that Brandeis would have welcomed a provision in the Federal Social Security law giving credit for contributions made only pursuant to a state plan of the Wisconsin type. But the prevailing philosophy, for better or for worse, was to the contrary, a philosophy influenced by the experience of social workers and the popular spread of insurance. Despite the disappointment, Brandeis did not hesitate to join in upholding the pooled-reserve plan as constitutional.[8]

He had other similar convictions which might have appeared whimsical or crotchety had they not derived from what were to him fundamental principles of a working capitalism. Consider for example so seemingly trivial a matter as fidelity insurance. He considered it, in a word, as an abomination — and the word is his — for to him it was the

very negation of managerial responsibility to di-
vest itself of the duty and the risk of knowing the
character of trusted employees. Yet I daresay no
one will be heard to suggest that in his judgments
on the bench fidelity insurance fared badly on that
account. The principle of informed vigilance as the
soul of business enterprise was likewise violated in
his view by the practice of large depositors, particularly public bodies, taking a pledge of assets
from a bank to secure their deposits. Not only was
the practice prejudicial to the ordinary unsecured
depositor — Brandeis liked to point out that the
familiar banking sign "Government Depositary"
was apt to be quite misleading to the small cus-
tomer — but in addition it removed an incentive
for vigilance on the part of government authorities
in supervising banks in which government deposits
were placed. He believed, for example, that a spectacular bank failure in New York might have been
averted had the state retained this incentive. On
the bench he did indeed write an opinion for the
Court holding that national banks lacked power to
secure the deposits of private customers by pledging assets; but he joined with the Court in interpreting an amendment to the National Banking Act
as validating retroactively the pledging of assets to

secure the deposits of states and their subdivisions.[9]

In constitutional law as well he was obliged on occasion to subordinate his deeply held convictions to the canons of his office. During the depression he kept a file, labeled with characteristic directness "Depression Cures." I am certain that far down on the list in his own evaluation came schemes for the limiting of production. And yet none of his opinions showed more laborious or earnest effort than his dissent in the *New State Ice* case, arguing for the authority of Oklahoma to limit access to the ice business by the issuance of certificates of convenience and necessity. Only a note of skepticism, uncommon in his opinions, served to betray his private judgment of the law:

The objections to the proposal are obvious and grave. The remedy might bring evils worse than the present disease. The obstacles to success seem insuperable. The economic and social sciences are largely uncharted seas. We have been none too successful in the modest essays in economic control already entered upon. The new proposal involves a vast extension of the area of control. Merely to acquire the knowledge essential as a basis for the exercise of this multitude of judgments would be a formidable task; and each of the thousands of these judgments would call for some measure of prophecy. Even more serious are the obstacles to success inherent in the demands which execution of the project would make upon human intelligence and upon the character of men. Man is weak and his judgment is at best fallible.

Yet the advances in the exact sciences and the achievements in invention remind us that the seemingly impossible sometimes happens. . . .

To stay experimentation in things social and economic is a grave responsibility. Denial of the right to experiment may be fraught with serious consequences to the Nation. It is one of the happy incidents of the federal system that a single courageous State may, if its citizens choose, serve as a laboratory; and try novel social and economic experiments without risk to the rest of the country. This Court has the power to prevent an experiment. We may strike down the statute which embodies it on the ground that, in our opinion, the measure is arbitrary, capricious or unreasonable. We have power to do this, because the due process clause has been held by the Court applicable to matters of substantive law as well as to matters of procedure. But in the exercise of this high power, we must be ever on our guard, lest we erect our prejudices into legal principles. If we would guide by the light of reason, we must let our minds be bold.[10]

At the following term he delivered another elaborate dissent, this time in support of the power of Florida to impose graduated taxes on chain stores proportionate to the number of counties in which they operated.[11] Here his legislative judgment coincided entirely with his judicial judgment, and the opinion was a labor of love; but it was no more zealous and thorough-going than the dissent of the term before.

An experiment which he watched with the utmost sympathy was the Tennessee Valley Authority. Like coöperatives, it provided a new form of enterprise in which the energies and imagination of large numbers of people could be enlisted; and it provided something of a measuring rod for more conventional forms of enterprise. When the first test came of the constitutional basis for the sale of commercial power by the Authority, a majority of the Court, led by Chief Justice Hughes, sustained the activity. While Brandeis by no means disagreed as a matter of constitutional law, he was of opinion that the shareholders' suit by which the question was presented was not a proper vehicle to reach the constitutional question, and he therefore concurred in the result, but on procedural grounds.[12] The opportunity to obtain a basic validation of TVA was less important to him than the maintenance of proper standards of judicial review.

And so we are led to look more closely into what I have called his insistence on jurisdictional and procedural observances.

(3) It has sometimes been said that Brandeis

was a liberal in social and economic thought and a conservative in matters of legal procedure. The truth is that his procedural attitudes were part and parcel of those qualities of mind which made him a liberal. He did indeed dissent alone from the promulgation of the federal rules of civil procedure. His reasons were not publicly stated, but they are not unknown. Partly he was unwilling to take responsibility for a complicated formulation to which he as well as other members of the Court had been able to give only limited consideration. Partly he was influenced by an apprehension that the rules might become as intricate as the codification of civil practice in New York, which was hardly to be preferred to the simple Massachusetts system under which he had practiced. Finally, the devotion to the federal principle which motivated his opinion in *Erie Railroad* v. *Tompkins*,[13] enforcing conformity to state rules of decision in the federal courts, led him likewise to reject the idea of nationalization of rules of procedure for the federal courts.

It is true also that he set himself firmly against declaratory judgments, yielding only when Congress authorized them "in cases of actual controversy." [14] One may venture to suggest that he was no more opposed to declaratory judgments for the staple business of state courts than he was to the adoption by state courts of many of the specific reforms in the federal rules of civil procedure. What he discerned in declaratory judgments was a device, only somewhat less objectionable than advisory opinions, which might be used to bring before the courts questions of the validity of statutes at what he regarded as a premature stage. It was too easy by these means to expose the legislative plant to the judicial blight before it had come to full fruition. The experience in some states had shown the truth of Laertes' words, "The canker galls the infants of the spring Too oft before their buttons are disclosed." What may appear in isolation to be surprisingly conservative responses to procedural reforms turn out to be phases of a pervading philosophy — the faithful maintenance of the federal balance and the fullest scope for experimentation by legislatures free of judicial constraint.

His respect for the spheres of competence of other organs of authority showed itself in his forbearance when sitting in judgment on the decisions of administrative agencies. But they forfeited their claim when they in turn failed to observe procedural guarantees. "The mere admission by an administrative tribunal," Brandeis said, "of matter which under the rules of evidence applicable to judicial proceedings would be deemed incompetent . . . or mere error in reasoning upon evidence introduced, does not invalidate an order. But where rates found by a regulatory body to be compensatory are attacked as being confiscatory, courts may enquire into the method by which its conclusion was reached. An order based upon a finding made without evidence . . . or upon a finding made upon evidence which clearly does not support it . . . is an arbitrary act against which courts afford relief." [15]

Moreover, procedures for challenging administrative orders must also be adequate. Brandeis wrote a number of opinions developing the theme that if a utility is obliged to violate an order to test its validity, the penalties for violation must not be oppressive, else no fair opportunity for challenge would be provided. Consequently he was prepared to enjoin the enforcement of such penalties even though the rate order should ultimately be held valid. He explained it in this way: "If upon final hearing the maximum rates fixed should be found not to be confiscatory, a permanent injunction should, nevertheless, issue to restrain enforcement of penalties accrued *pendent lite,* provided that it also be found that the plaintiff had reasonable ground to contest them as being confiscatory." [16] Parenthetically, may not this technique suggest a suitable procedure to govern injunctions against threatened prosecution for exercising rights of speech? May not the threat of prosecution itself be a cloud on speech which is an illegitimate deterrent where the prohibition though ultimately found valid was at least questionable? That is, in proper cases may there not be a guaranteed interim period of freedom from restraint pending a final decision?

Brandeis himself recognized, in another context, that the subject matter regulated should color the procedure on review. He put it candidly in his great concurring opinion in the *St. Joseph Stock Yards* case where he drew a distinction "between the right to liberty of person and other constitutional rights. . . . A citizen who claims that his liberty is being infringed is entitled, upon habeas corpus, to the opportunity of a judicial determination of the facts. And, so highly is this liberty prized, that the opportunity must be accorded to any resident of the United States who claims to be a citizen. . . . But a multitude of decisions tells us that when dealing with property a much more liberal rule applies.

They show that due process of law does not always entitle an owner to have the correctness of findings of fact reviewed by a court. . . ." [17]

Candid as he was in asserting a difference between elementary interests of personality and other interests, procedural observances were bound to be enforced in either case. His opinion in Anita Whitney's case is one of the classics in the literature of freedom of speech; it is sometimes forgotten, however, that he concurred in affirming the conviction because of failure to present adequately in the lower court the defense that there was no clear and present danger. [18]

Late in his career, in the *Senn* case, he stated by way of dictum that "Members of a union might, without special statutory authorization by a state, make known the facts of a labor dispute, for freedom of speech is guaranteed by the Federal Constitution." [19] But he was far from asserting that the admixture of elements of speech with elements of a labor controversy puts the matter beyond the pale of regulation. For immediately following the dictum he added, "The state may, in the exercise of its police power, regulate the methods and means of publicity as well as the use of public streets." There is no reason to believe that he abandoned the considered views which he had expressed twenty years earlier in his dissent in the *Duplex* case, where he would have permitted labor unions to conduct a boycott of a manufacturer and his customers, adding a caveat:

Because I have come to the conclusion that both the common law of a State and a statute of the United States declare the right of industrial combatants to push their struggle to the limits of the justification of self-interest, I do not wish to be understood as attaching any constitutional or moral sanction to that right. All rights are derived from the purposes of the society in which they exist; above all rights rises duty to the community. The conditions developed in industry may be such that those engaged in it cannot continue their struggle without danger to the community. But it is not for judges to determine whether such conditions exist, nor is it their function to set the limits of permissible contest and to declare the duties which the new situation demands. This is the function of the legislature which, while limiting individual and group rights of aggression and defense, may substitute processes of justice for the more primitive method of trial by combat.[20]

His respect for the competence of legislatures and boards to govern was not limited to his abstention after they had acted. More than once he insisted that the courts refrain from intervening at all because the problem lent itself potentially to full-scale administrative treatment far better than to fragmentary judicial control. Two of his most suggestive opinions, both in dissent, struck this note. In the celebrated case of *Associated Press* v. *International News Service* [21] he would have had the Court do nothing to restrain the pirating of the plaintiff's news bulletins by the defendant, since in granting the relief the Court was creating new rights of property without the competence to impose on the successful party suitable obligations to the public in the dissemination of news. In *Pennsylvania* v. *West Virginia* [22] he would not have lent the aid of the Court to the plaintiff state to restrain the enforcement of a West Virginia law limiting the out-of-state shipment of natural gas; for here too the Court was without adequate standards to deal constructively with the problem of equitable apportionment of the industrial resources of a state. Even the traditional instrument of a court of equity, the conditional decree, may be much less adequate than a legislative standard administered by an agency continuously responsible and informed by expert judgment.

This pervading concern with the fitness of the members of the body politic for their respective tasks, this genuinely organic conception of government, encompassed the Supreme Court itself. Consequently such technical issues as the distinction between obligatory jurisdiction on appeal as against discretionary jurisdiction on certiorari assumed for Brandeis the importance of first principles.[23] He was a firm believer in limiting the jurisdiction of the Supreme Court on every front, and he would not be seduced by the quixotic temptation to right every fancied wrong which was paraded before him. The time was always out of joint but he was not born alone to set it right. Grievances set out in petitions for certiorari were examined with great dispatch, and if the petitions did not carry on their face compelling reasons for granting them they were promptly marked for denial. Husbanding his time and energies as if the next day were to be his last, he steeled himself, like a scientist in the service of man, against the enervating distraction of the countless tragedies he was not meant to relieve. His concern for jurisdictional and procedural limits reflected, on the technical level, an essentially Stoic philosophy. For like Epictetus he recognized "the impropriety of being emotionally affected by what is not under one's control."[24]

And so we are led to what I have called the final

aspect of his morality of mind, his rejection of sentimentality.

(4) He was, to be sure, a humanitarian, as admirers are fond of saying. But he was so in a Lincolnesque sense, even as he bore a certain resemblance to Lincoln in countenance and bearing. His devotion to a harmonious federal union, like Lincoln's, could take precedence over his immediate emotional attachments. Within the Constitution he found resources for a strengthened federalism which had been imperfectly tapped. Among these was the full faith and credit clause, offering a means of cementing the states without superseding their authority by national legislation. He saw an opportunity to allay friction and avoid overlapping of state powers through the fuller application of this clause, and he was not deterred by the circumstance that the result in specific cases would distress his natural sympathies. In one case he insisted that an injured workman could not recover from his employer under the law of another state if the state of employment had made its compensation act the exclusive remedy.[25] In a second case he ruled that the beneficiary suing under a life insurance policy could not take advantage of the law

of her present home if the law of the state where the policy was issued and where the insured had resided gave the insurance company a defense on ground of the insured's misrepresentation.[26] In a third case he maintained that a minor child could not recover additional support from her father under the law of her present residence if a judgment for support previously rendered at her father's domicile was unmodifiable by the law of that state.[27] Each of these opinions was by no means compelled by text or precedent; indeed the first of them has subsequently been overruled, and the third provoked a dissent from Justices Stone and Cardozo. Yet Brandeis was prepared to reject the claims, almost literally, of a workman, a widow and an orphan in pursuance of what seemed to him to be a more harmonious federalism.

No one would have been more entitled, or less inclined, to echo the words of the German historian, "I have spent sleepless nights that others might rest." Sometimes humanitarianism requires a hard choice between man and men. Jonathan Swift could say that he hated man but loved Pope and Bolingbroke. But in a great judge, as in all who have successfully shouldered the responsibility of power, sentiments of affection yield to devotion to the larger cause. To an unsentimental judge hard cases may make good law.

There was finally in Brandeis a deep institutional sense concerning his Court. It showed itself in small details. He took a paradoxical pleasure in receiving little critical comments from his brethren on drafts of his opinions, for he accepted these as welcome evidence that his colleagues were alert to their corporate responsibility. When he appeared before a Senate committee with Chief Justice Hughes and Mr. Justice Van Devanter to testify on a bill to amend the Court's jurisdiction, and was asked to add his testimony to that of his two brethren, he simply responded, "Mr. Chairman and gentlemen, the subject has been discussed so fully by the Chief Justice and Mr. Justice Van Devanter that I think I can aid you best by saying I agree absolutely with everything they have said." [28] It is quite possible that in his last official act — retirement rather than resignation — he was motivated in his choice by the fact that two of his brethren had but recently chosen retirement and he was unwilling to make an invidious departure from their practice.

His sense of institutional solidarity was stronger than his attachment to any one of his colleagues, even to Holmes. For while he avoided any act that might impair the standing of the Court he did not indulge in monotonous or slavish agreement with his senior associate. Their disagreements were not frequent but they were not unimportant. In two celebrated cases Holmes was led by his guiding canons to support action by a state which Brandeis regarded as an infringement of constitutional liberty. In *Gilbert* v. *Minnesota*[29] Holmes concurred in sustaining a conviction under a state law for discouraging enlistment in the armed forces, while Brandeis regarded the statute as too broadly drawn and in any event not applicable in a sphere where Congress alone should have authority to take protective measures. In *Meyer* v. *Nebraska*[30] the Court held that a state could not forbid the teaching of modern foreign languages in private schools in the elementary grades. Brandeis concurred without opinion while Holmes dissented. These two cases raised in perplexing form the dilemma facing a judge who is faithful both to the principle of local self-government and to that of freedom of the mind. In the ultimate test Holmes as a judge set a higher value on freedom of experimentation by the state, Brandeis on freedom of experimentation in ideas. The division in these cases ought to be a sufficient caveat that the light of liberalism does not point its shafts in only one direction.

Other significant divisions occurred. In *Casey* v. *United States*[31] Holmes wrote for the Court sustaining the conviction of a defendant under the Narcotics Act despite evidence in the record that the offense was committed as the result of enticement by persons under the direction of the government. Brandeis regarded the evidence as so challenging that the Court of its own motion should have directed an acquittal even though the defense of entrapment was not relied on by counsel in the case. Procedural abuses in law enforcement were for him matters that involved the integrity of the Court itself. In *Hughes* v. *Gault*[32] Holmes delivered the opinion of the Court holding that in proceedings for removal of a person under indictment from one federal district to another the accused was not constitutionally entitled to a hearing and that the statutory implication of a hearing had been satisfied. Brandeis took the position that the Commissioner's refusal to hear certain evidence of the accused going to the issue of probable cause did not merely constitute error but "deprived the petitioner of his liberty without due process of law in violation of the Fifth Amendment, because he was denied a fair hearing." It is worth recalling that in this case the offense for which the accused was indicted was a violation of the antitrust laws, and so we have the spectacle of Holmes, notoriously skeptical of the Sherman Act, lending the aid of the Court to its enforcement, with Brandeis, the friend of antitrust legislation, interposing an obstacle to enforcement. Cases of this sort must trouble those engaged in the occupation of pigeonholing judges. Is this to be classified as an antitrust case, or a criminal case, or forsooth a civil liberties case; and whose was the liberal vote? I leave the answer to those who indulge in the tabulating enterprise.

We return from this digression on Brandeis and Holmes to Brandeis's feeling for the Court as an institution. The sentiment was publicly, though implicitly, reflected in his opinions. They were uniformly addressed to problems and not to persons. They were self-contained, the expression of a judge content to leave his reasoned judgments to the second thought of time and his successors. Not infrequently the preparation of a dissenting opinion was forgone because the demands of other items of work prevented an adequate treatment, but with the promise to himself that another occasion would be taken when circumstances were more propitious.

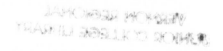

If his opinions are firm and poised it is because they reflect an inner security and confidence and faith in the power of dispassionate reason.

I have stressed some elements of Brandeis's thought which are apt to be minimized in the popular picture of a liberal judge — his insistence on knowledge, his rejection of opportunism, his insistence on procedural and jurisdictional observances, and his rejection of sentimentality, and in addition his devotion to the Court while preserving his own intellectual independence. Two other elements in his thinking are more obvious to the public eye and are also part of his liberalism but need less emphasis because they are more familiar. I mean, first, his attitude toward *stare decisis*, and, second, his expression of social and economic ideas.

It is of course true that he did not regard *stare decisis* as an inexorable command, though he also confessed that "in most matters it is more important that the applicable rule of law be settled than that it be settled right." [33] It was in constitutional cases that he gave freest scope for reconsideration of doctrine, for the only alternative is the heroic process of constitutional amendment. Where the legislature was left free to overcome a decision there was less pressing responsibility on the Court to reconsider,

though I do not mean to suggest that he drew a hard and fast line between overruling constitutional doctrine and overruling statutory construction. But it is significant that in the most spectacular overruling of recent years, in *Erie Railroad Company* v. *Tompkins*,[34] where the century-old precedent of *Swift* v. *Tyson* was discarded, Brandeis felt impelled to explain that the issue went beyond the mere construction of the Rules of Decision Act of 1790. He ventured to say that the whole course of decision following *Swift* v. *Tyson*, whereby federal courts had declared the common law independently of state decisions, was unconstitutional. It would have been preferable, I believe, simply to treat the question as one of interpreting the Rules of Decision Act or as one of self-limitation on the part of federal courts in developing the common law. Yet Brandeis's standards of *stare decisis* could not easily be satisfied without putting the matter in terms of reexamining a constitutional question.

The other familiar element in Brandeis's opinions is their employment as a vehicle for his social and economic thought. In the main, his essays in this area were an elucidation of legislation which he was glad to accept. To be sure, he was an abler exponent than the legislators themselves; they may have marveled at times at the unsuspected depth of their own thinking. Within the confines of the judicial office Brandeis was thus an educator of the first rank. But judges are educators only by the way, as he well knew. It was to education in the general sense, rather than to judges, that he looked for the realization of his hopes for society. In his view the great depression reflected a failure not of the laws or of the courts or even primarily of economic institutions but essentially of education. The ill-starred NRA, which he joined in declaring unconstitutional, and whose mistakes were instructive, should have been created, he once remarked, as a bureau in the Office of Education. On a lower level, when he found that more than half of his law clerks were engaged in teaching, he said with satisfaction, "Now I have a majority." Even his attachment to federalism had about it a considerable feeling for its educational value.[35] And though it is sometimes the fashion to regard the federal principle as archaic and obscurantist, are not our successes and failures in its operation of vital concern to a world groping toward some form of federalism in order to save itself?

You will note that the portrait I have sketched does not resemble the typical picture of the liberal which many hold today. Our age is contentious and frenetic, inclined to distrust the force of standards which one's adversaries may choose to ignore, inclined to seize its own innings and impatiently mark up victories and defeats day by day. And yet who can say that we may safely stake our vision of the future on the accumulation of little triumphs of the day unless they are earned by what I have ventured to call morality of the mind — by understanding, self-restraint, and the even-handed application of principle? The liberalism of Brandeis the judge was marked by these qualities, and it may have meaning therefore beyond his office and his time, for our day and for the day we shall not see.

III. "Judge and Company" in Constitutional Law

IT IS NOTORIOUS that the lawyer has been the most abused of men in the literature of all nations. Perhaps the most compendious abuse was delivered by Plato when he put into the mouth of Socrates these words:

[The lawyer] is a servant, and is disputing about a fellow-servant before his master, who is seated, and has the cause in his hands; the trial is never about some indifferent matter, but always concerns himself; and often he has to run for his life. The consequence has been, that he has become keen and shrewd; he has learned how to flatter his master in word and indulge him in deed; but his soul is small and unrighteous. His slavish condition has deprived him of growth and uprightness and independence; dangers and fears, which were too much for his truth and honesty, came upon him in early years, when the tenderness of youth was unequal to them, and he has been driven into crooked ways; from the first he has practised deception and retaliation, and has become stunted and warped. And so he has passed out of youth into manhood, having no soundness in him; and is now, as he thinks, a master in wisdom. Such is the lawyer, Theodorus.[1]

This would furnish a text for a good many lectures. But my interest presently is with the idea expressed at the beginning of the passage, that the lawyer is a servant disputing before his master seated on the bench. So far as American constitutional law is concerned, it might almost as well be said that the judge is a servant seated before his masters. At any rate, I think that the truth in this regard was perceived by Jeremy Bentham when he said, "The law is not made by judge alone, but by judge and company."

The company who share the lawmaking activity of Supreme Court judges include at least the lower tribunals as well as counsel. The deference paid to the views of other judicial or administrative officers will necessarily be affected by the regard in which they are held. Such deference, as Holmes said of continuity with the past, is not a duty, only a necessity — a psychological necessity. Judge Wyzanski has remarked on the weight which Judge A. N. Hand gives to the opinions of "strong" courts.[2] Lord Bowen, to take the opposite case, is said to have

observed, "To have a judgment of my brother Keke-
wich in your favor is certainly a misfortune, but
not necessarily fatal." One may be permitted to
wonder whether the decision in *Betts* v. *Brady*,[3]
holding the appointment of counsel for indigent
criminal defendants in state courts not to be an
invariable constitutional requirement, would have
been the same had the opinion of the court below
been written by someone less highly esteemed than
Chief Judge Bond of Maryland, who is referred to
by name in Mr. Justice Roberts's opinion no less
than fifteen times. One may speculate, too, whether
the decision in the Japanese evacuation cases [4]
would have been the same had the final administrative determination been made by someone whose
judgment was less deeply respected than Secretary
Stimson's.

Of course we are aware of the indebtedness of
judges to the briefs and arguments of counsel in
the preparation of opinions. Every schoolboy knows
how large a part of Daniel Webster's arguments before the Supreme Court found their way into the
opinions of Marshall. It seems that Webster was
not content to risk his achievement in this regard
to the discernment of future historians. He was at
pains to point out during his lifetime the extent of

his contribution to the judicial utterances of the great Chief Justice. In *Gibbons* v. *Ogden* Webster was co-counsel with William Wirt, arguing successfully against the New York steamboat monopoly. After the decision, Webster is said to have observed to a friend:

The opinion of the Court, as rendered by the Chief Justice, was little else than a recital of my argument. The Chief Justice told me that he had little to do but to repeat that argument, as that covered the whole ground. And, which was a little curious, he never referred to the fact that Mr. Wirt had made an argument. He did not speak of it once. . . . That was very singular. It was an accident, I think. Mr. Wirt was a great lawyer, and a great man. But sometimes a man gets a kink and doesn't hit right.[5]

On at least one occasion, it seems to me, the argument of Daniel Webster had a curiously repelling rather than an attracting force with the Court. In the Rhode Island rebellion case, *Luther* v. *Borden*,[6] Webster represented the officers of the established government who were sued for trespass in putting down the activities of the rival government which the radicals of the day, the Loco-Foco party, were trying to set up. The argument in the Supreme Court took a broad range. It dealt with the very principles of representative government and the place of revolution in our constitutional system. This was certainly strong meat for a court of law to be asked to chew, and Webster almost at the outset of his argument frankly said so:

The aspect of the case is, as I have said, novel. It may perhaps give vivacity and variety to judicial investigations. It may relieve the drudgery of perusing briefs, demurrers, and pleas in bar, bills in equity and answers, and introduce topics which give sprightliness, freshness, and something of an uncommon public interest to proceedings in courts of law.

. . . It is said, and truly said, that the case involves the consideration and discussion of what are the true principles of government in our American system of public liberty. This is very right. The case does involve these questions, and harm can never come from their discussion, especially when such discussion is addressed to reason and not to passion; when it is had before magistrates and lawyers, and not before excited masses out of doors. I agree entirely that the case does raise considerations, somewhat extensive, of the true character of our American system of popular liberty; and although I am constrained to differ from the learned counsel who opened the cause for the plaintiff in error, on the principles and character of that American liberty, and upon the true characteristics of that American system on which changes of the government and constitution, if they become necessary, are to be made, yet I agree with him that this case does present them for consideration.[7]

The case of *Luther* v. *Borden* is now a leading case on what the federal courts will *not* decide. The court regarded the broad questions, so sprightly and fascinating to the student of government, as not within the competence of the judiciary. Whether a purported government is the *de jure* government of a state, and whether it is a representative form of government as guaranteed to the states by the Constitution, are questions which must be left to the other branches of the national government to decide. They are political, not justiciable, questions. It would be tempting to say that Webster had over-reached himself in his argument, except for the fact that, in the outcome of the case, his clients prevailed, since the court professed itself to be in no position to grant relief against the defendant officers.

These are instances in which the dramatic quality of the advocate's argument has played its part. But there are other and subtler ways in which counsel have a crucial rôle to play in the shaping of constitutional law.

Perhaps the most significant single feature of our system of judicial review of the constitutionality of legislation is the fact that the function is carried out in the course of an ordinary lawsuit. The consequence is that many important constitutional questions are decided in litigation which in form is entirely private. The validity of the gold-clause legislation as applied to private debts was decided in a case brought by a bondholder against a railroad on a coupon for $22.50.[8]

The result of this practice has not always been fortunate. Sometimes issues have been decided of the gravest importance which a court, if better advised, could with propriety have left undecided, and which the judgment of history suggests should have been left for decision at a later date and perhaps by other arbiters. I am thinking, for example, of two cases which Chief Justice Hughes, in his Columbia lectures during his interregnum, referred to as among the Court's self-inflicted wounds — the *Dred Scott* case and the *Income Tax* cases.[9] No graver issue was ever decided by the Supreme Court than that in the *Dred Scott* case; and it was presented in circumstances which suggested that the Court had no business dealing with it at all. A colorable transfer of ownership of Scott from his Missouri master to a brother-in-law in New York was relied on to create diversity of citizenship between Scott and the defendant and so to provide a basis for relitigating in a federal circuit court the issue which a Missouri court had decided adversely to Scott. This maneuver proved successful, so far as jurisdiction was concerned, and the case was presented on an agreed statement of facts, though it would seem that, in a genuine lawsuit, evidence would have been introduced to show the character of the transfer and to indicate that Dred Scott was simply a pawn in a jurisdictional game.

In the *Income Tax* cases as well the self-inflicted wound could have been averted. The plaintiff stockholder could show irreparable injury through payment of the tax by his corporation only if the corporation would have been without a remedy at law to recover the tax. Such a remedy was open to it if it paid the tax under protest. All that was necessary for the protection of the stockholder was a decision requiring the corporation to pay under protest and thus protecting its rights in the event that in another proceeding the tax should be held unconstitutional.[10]

These are cases in which counsel were perhaps too eager for the settlement of burning issues. A different sort of danger is also present in such cases — the danger that one side will not have an adequate interest in the presentation of the case. Whether or not a stockholder's suit will produce a real contest, as apparently it did in the *Pollock* case, depends on the attitude of counsel. The Trust Company may be thought not to have had a passionate interest in sustaining the income tax levied upon it, though Mr. Carter, who argued for the validity of the tax, had no doubt the greatest personal interest in achieving a victory over his rival at the bar, Mr. Choate. Other cases are brought to test the validity of legislation where the element of professional rivalry may not be an adequate safeguard. One common type of regulation is the prohibition of shipments of certain goods in interstate commerce. A familiar form of litigation under such a statute is a suit by a shipper against a public carrier to compel it to transport the goods. The carrier defends on the ground that the statute forbids it and that the statute is valid.[11] But it may fairly be questioned whether the carrier is deeply interested in sustaining a law which will cut down the volume of shipments that would otherwise be made.

Whether or not the government was represented at all in these purely private lawsuits depended on whether the government had notice that the suit had been brought, and whether participation as a friend of the court was thought advisable. It was not until 1937 that the government was given a right to become a party in any suit where the constitutionality of an Act of Congress is drawn in question. The Judiciary Act of 1937 enables the government not only to present argument to the court, but to participate from the very beginning in the making of the record, so that questions of collusion, lack of standing of the plaintiff, or the relevance of economic and other data to the constitutional issue, may be reflected in the record.

The Act of 1937 provides an opportunity for government counsel to make their contribution to the conduct of every case involving the validity of a federal statute. Just what contribution can be made? I shall deal with this question in three aspects — the *what,* the *how,* and the *when,* of constitutional litigation.

What the data are upon which the court may draw in deciding a case is largely the responsibility of counsel. Counsel must provide, to use a phrase of Mr. John W. Davis, the implements of decision. Probably the most notable contribution to the lawyer's technique in constitutional cases was the so-called Brandeis brief submitted in the Oregon hours-of-labor-for-women case.[12] It drew on reports of public investigating committees, books and articles by medical authorities and social workers, and the

practice of legislatures here and abroad. This type
of brief has been in fairly common use ever since.
It has been particularly utilized by the government. It is one of the few inventions in legal technique that can be identified in a profession which
is not notable for wandering off the beaten path.
The invention has been widely and justly acclaimed.
Yet it raises a number of very real problems which
I shall simply suggest.

In the first place, it may be questioned whether
the advocate arguing in favor of the validity of a
statute should take the burden of supporting it by a
mass of factual data instead of relying on the presumption of constitutionality. Is not the government advocate who submits a Brandeis brief tempting the court to decide the case without the benefit
of the presumption — to decide it, that is, as if the
burden of sustaining the statute were upon the pro-
ponent? This objection needs to be raised, but it
seems to me that it can be answered. The presumption of constitutionality need not be lost sight of; but
even a court which relies on the presumption in sustaining a statute does so more confidently and more
comfortably if some factual foundation has been
established for the validity of the law. And I take it
that it is the function of counsel not merely to pro-

vide the legal doctrine for deciding the case his
way, but to make the court feel comfortable in doing
so.

Perhaps a more serious objection to the so-called
Brandeis brief is that the data presented ought to
be placed in the record and not left simply for the
brief. If the data are presented for the record, there
will be an opportunity for impeaching them and
offering countervailing data. The answer to this is,
I suppose, that the data are offered not for the truth
of the facts asserted but only to establish that responsible persons have made the assertions and hold
the opinions which are disclosed. That is to say, the
court need not decide whether, for example, filled
milk which substitutes cocoanut oil for butter fat is
or is not deceptive or detrimental to health; the
court need only decide whether there is responsible
opinion that it is so. Consequently, the introduction
of countervailing evidence would be immaterial.
This serves to show the almost insuperable burden
placed on the opponents of economic legislation to
overcome the effect of data adduced in support. The
opponents must show that the opinion in support of
the legislation is wholly untenable. Arguing as counsel in the Oregon minimum-wage case, Brandeis put
the point in extreme terms:

In answer to the question, whether this brief contains also all the data opposed to minimum-wage law, I want to say this: I conceive it to be absolutely immaterial what may be said against such laws. Each one of these statements contained in the brief in support of the contention that this is wise legislation, might upon further investigation be found to be erroneous, each conclusion of fact may be found afterwards to be unsound — and yet the constitutionality of the act would not be affected thereby. This court is not burdened with the duty of passing upon the disputed question whether the legislature of Oregon was wise or unwise, or probably wise or unwise, in enacting this law. The question is merely whether, as has been stated, you can see that the legislators had no ground on which they could, as reasonable men, deem this legislation appropriate to abolish or mitigate the evils believed to exist or apprehended. If you cannot find that, the law must stand.[13]

It does seem, however, that by virtue of the very magnitude of this burden, there might well be required an opportunity to impeach, by cross-examination or otherwise, the evidence presented in support of constitutionality. This cannot be done effectively by a reply brief. It needs to be done in the trial court as part of the record. I should add at this point that the practice of the government has by no means been limited to the placing of such data in the briefs. In many of the most important constitu-

tional cases, the material has actually been introduced into the record. Sometimes this has been done
by calling expert witnesses — government economists or outside economists — or by introducing into
the record publications of responsible authorities.
This was done, for example, in the Guffey Coal Act
case,[14] where voluminous testimony was taken regarding the history of labor disturbances in the coal
industry and the effect on the volume of shipments
and competitive conditions in the industry. It was
done in the PWA cases,[15] where testimony was taken
regarding studies made by the Bureau of Labor
Statistics on the effectiveness of a public works program in the relief of unemployment. It was done at
great length in the omnibus TVA case,[16] where a
galaxy of engineers — military, civil and hydraulic
— testified on both sides concerning the usefulness
of the TVA projects for navigation, flood control,
and national defense.

One final objection to the so-called Brandeis brief
is that it places an inappropriate task on counsel. Is
the adversary method the most suitable one for dealing with economic data? Someone has said that there
are three sides to every lawsuit — my side, your side,
and the truth. Should the responsibility for develop-

ing the background facts be placed on counsel, or should it be borne by some disinterested source? Should there be established for the courts something equivalent to the legislative reference service organized in a number of states for the benefit of the legislature? This would perhaps be a more radical innovation than the Brandeis brief itself, and yet it is not altogether fanciful. We owe much of our commercial law to the boldness of Lord Mansfield in seeking advice from experienced merchants regarding mercantile practices. The English admiralty courts have utilized the services of retired mariners drawn from the Royal Navy and the Merchant Marine — the celebrated "elder brethren of Trinity House." Some of our courts are beginning to employ disinterested medical and psychiatric advisers. The great difficulty with this idea in constitutional litigation is that the experts would be tempted to intrude their views on the merits of the legislation instead of helping the court to understand other people's views. Perhaps the right place for non-legal experts in constitutional law is in the legislative process. If records of hearings and committee reports, particularly in state legislatures, were more illuminating and accessible, the task of the advocate in court would be simpler, and the court itself would be more disposed to display that basic judicial virtue, modesty.

When we pass from *what* is presented to *how* it is presented, the rôle of counsel is even more striking. To some degree, the choice of the lawsuit which is to be the test case is in counsel's hands. Should a case be chosen which will present the issues narrowly or broadly? Should an all-out contest be risked or should a more limited engagement be fought?

The long-drawn-out litigation over the TVA was a clash of two views of constitutional warfare. The power companies endeavored to attack what they described as the whole "plan and program" of the TVA, as revealed in speeches, official studies and promotional literature, dealing with the development of a great river system and electrification of the Valley. One of these documents to which the power companies were fond of pointing bore the lyrical title "There'll be Shouting in the Valley." The TVA, on the other hand, insisted that all that was in issue in the case was the lawfulness of certain hydroelectric structures already completed and the sale of power under contracts already in existence or definitely contemplated. The first case was in form a stockholders' suit by preferred stock-

holders against the Alabama Power Company and
the TVA to enjoin the performance of a contract
which the company had made with the Authority.
The company was controlled by Commonwealth &
Southern, which owned all the common stock and
which had arranged for the contract — or truce, as
it was sometimes called — with the TVA. This ac-
counts for the fact that the suit was begun by
preferred rather than by common stockholders. The
contract provided for the sale of transmission lines
to TVA, and a division of territory between the
company and TVA in Alabama. All the electric
energy which the TVA would need in order to serve
the territory ceded to it by the company in Alabama
could be supplied by the generators at Wilson Dam.
That dam was begun in 1918 and completed in
1925, long before the New Deal and TVA came
upon the scene. In fact, it was authorized originally
as a military project to provide power for the manu-
facture of nitrates. The counsel for the complainants
regarded the case as one to test the whole plan and
policy, as I have said, of the TVA. Counsel for the
TVA maintained that what was in issue was simply
the validity of Wilson Dam and the contractual ar-
rangement for the sale of power from that dam to
municipalities in the area.

The district court granted a broad injunction against the TVA, with numerous findings and conclusions regarding the development of the entire Tennessee River as contemplated under the TVA Act. But the court made a finding, fatal to its own conception of the case, that Wilson Dam would supply all the power necessary to serve the customers in the territory formerly served by the Alabama Power Company. That finding became of critical importance on appeal. When Chief Justice Hughes asked counsel for the Power Company what the precise issue in the case was, counsel replied that it was the plan and program of the TVA; whereupon the Chief Justice said, "It is the validity of a contract, is it not?" With that definition of the issue, the result of the case was hardly in doubt. The lawfulness of Wilson Dam was sustained under the war powers and the power over commerce on navigable waters, and the purchase of transmission lines for the sale of power from the dam was sustained as a legitimate means of disposing of government-owned property — that is, the water power — which is inevitably created by the maintenance of the dam and the flow of water over it.[17] There is a treasure in the waters, as government counsel put it, and the Constitution does not require that it go to waste.

This was, of course, only the preliminary skirmish, though it seemed to lay the groundwork for upholding the dams constructed under TVA auspices, with their generators and transmission lines. The strategy and counter-strategy became more subtle. The power companies now made sure that they would have a case presenting the TVA program in its broadest scope. They brought together nineteen companies, serving the southeastern United States, in a huge omnibus suit challenging all phases of the TVA power activities. This suit took a curious course before it was finally decided in the Supreme Court. As a matter of fact it started out not as one suit but as two identical ones. One was filed in the federal court for northern Alabama and the other in a state court in Tennessee. They were identical bills of complaint and were filed on the same day. This maneuver reflected uncertainty regarding venue. The TVA statute provides that the legal residence of the TVA is at Muscle Shoals, Alabama. Doubtless counsel for the power companies feared that suit would have to be brought in Alabama, or at least that a suit elsewhere would run the risk of eventual dismissal on venue or jurisdictional grounds. Nevertheless, the power companies were anxious to try a forum other than

Alabama and the Fifth Circuit, where the Court of Appeals had ruled adversely to them in the stockholders' case. Their plan evidently was to retain the Alabama suit simply as an anchor to windward while actively pursuing the Tennessee suit. The TVA met these tactics by attempting to bring on the Alabama suit for a prompt hearing on a motion to dismiss the bill of complaint, while filing an answer and moving slowly in the Tennessee case.

At this juncture the power companies decided to dismiss the Alabama suit voluntarily rather than risk its becoming the test case, and so they staked everything on the Tennessee proceeding, trusting that it would not be dismissed for lack of jurisdiction. They had very adroitly brought it in a state court in Tennessee, thus forcing the TVA to take the initiative in removing it to a federal court. By removing it, the TVA was barred from objecting in the federal court that the venue of the action was not properly laid in Tennessee. The TVA had one counter-move, which was ingenious but inadequate. Though objection to venue was lost by removal, lack of "jurisdiction" of the state court could still be set up, for the jurisdiction of a federal court on removal is derivative. The TVA argued that under Tennessee law an action against a public agency could be brought only in the courts of the agency's legal headquarters, which would be Alabama in this case. Had this argument been effective, the companies, which had deliberately instituted the case in the state rather than federal court in order to force a waiver of venue, would have been hoist by their own petard. Unfortunately for the cause of poetic justice, but I daresay properly, the Tennessee law was held not to support the TVA's argument *in extremis*.

The result of all these maneuvers was that the case was finally established in a federal court in Tennessee before a single judge. He granted a sweeping preliminary injunction against TVA; the TVA appealed to the circuit court of appeals. That court reversed the preliminary injunction and sent the case back for trial.[18] Meanwhile, however, Congress and the President had been wrestling with the so-called reorganization of the federal judiciary, less politely known as the court-packing plan. That plan, of course, never became law, but out of it grew the Judiciary Act of 1937, which contained a provision that a three-judge court must be called when an injunction is sought against the enforcement of a federal statute on constitutional grounds. By the time the TVA case was remanded to the

trial court, this provision was in force, and hence
the district court judge who granted the injunction
now found himself flanked by two associates. After
a lengthy trial, the three-judge court ruled in favor
of the TVA, with some adverse findings by the judge
who had first sat in the case.

It is always tempting to look back on history and
speculate on what would have happened to the
face of the world if Cleopatra's nose had been half
an inch longer or if the Germans had kept their right
flank stronger in the drive on Paris in 1914. If the
power companies had not asked for a preliminary
injunction, there would have been no basis for an
intermediate appeal and the case might have been
tried before the single judge and decided finally by
him in favor of the power companies with appropriate findings before the three-judge-court provision was enacted into law. At any rate, the companies were defeated in the three-judge court and
appealed to the Supreme Court. The TVA maintained throughout the case that the power companies had no standing to object to competition,
whether the TVA, in the abstract, was or was not
constitutional. In the Supreme Court it was this
defense which prevailed.[19] Thus technically the
Supreme Court did not give us a decision on the

validity of the entire TVA power program. Yet I cannot help believing that the detailed findings of the three-judge court in support of the validity of the TVA as a co-ordinated navigation, flood control and hydroelectric project made it more comfortable for the Supreme Court to dismiss the power companies' case on what might appear to be somewhat technical grounds.

The TVA litigation is not the only illustration of jockeying for position in constitutional lawsuits. An even more vivid instance occurred in the holding-company litigation. The interests opposed to the Holding Company Act were anxious to secure as early as possible a sweeping decision declaring the whole scheme of regulation unconstitutional. They were on the alert for a case which would lend itself to this purpose. The government, on the other hand, and in particular the Securities and Exchange Commission which had the responsibility of administering the act, were anxious to confine the first case under the act to the question of the duty of utilities to register with the Commission. The other provisions of the act — the so-called control provisions, relating to issuance of securities, acquisition of property, intercorporate loans, simplification of holding company structure, and the like — would thus be left for decision as cases should arise in the course of action taken by the SEC against particular companies. The SEC, moreover, was anxious that the first case should involve a relatively large and representative system, so that the practices which led to the enactment of the statute could be fully and fairly presented.

The utilities believed that they had found a case suitable in all respects for their purposes in the bankruptcy proceedings involving a relatively small holding company in the Maryland federal court.[20] One possibility of a quick and broad decision, without the hindrance of having the government as a party to the suit (for this was prior to the 1937 act), was simply that the trustee in bankruptcy might ask the court for instructions regarding the validity of the act in order to direct the trustee whether or not to comply. In a similar case in the Delaware federal court, Judge Nields refused to give such instructions, stating that it was an attempt to secure a decision striking down an act of Congress in the absence of those who were responsible for administering it.[21] Such a course, he said, would violate accepted canons of judicial procedure. To be sure, such constitutional decisions had frequently been given in the absence of government representation;

but here there was the special factor that the case did not seem to contain the safeguards of an adversary proceeding.

In the Maryland case, counsel were more careful. They took pains to see that there would be adverse claims made in the bankruptcy proceedings with respect to the validity of the statute. One bondholder, a corporation owning $150,000 in first lien bonds of the debtor, took the position that its interest would best be served by an outright liquidation of the company. It maintained that the Holding Company Act would require a liquidation because no reorganization of the system would be possible under the simplification provisions of the statute. Consequently, its counsel was in the position of arguing for the validity of the statute. The opposing side was taken in an intervening petition by another creditor who owned $2500 in bonds of the debtor. He agreed that the Holding Company Act would require liquidation and prevent reorganization; but he alleged that he desired a reorganization. His interest, therefore, was in having the statute declared unconstitutional.

At this juncture the Securities and Exchange Commission, through its counsel, came on the scene and urged the district court not to pass on the constitutional questions in this proceeding. They argued that such a decision would be premature since the time for registration had not yet arrived and the Commission had taken no action regarding the company; that the facts concerning this holding-company system were not adequately disclosed in the agreed statement; that counsel on both sides had joined in construing the Holding Company Act as preventing reorganization, a doubtful construction which the Commission should have an opportunity to consider in administrative proceedings relating to this company; and, finally, that it did not appear that the interests of the respective creditors were genuinely adverse. The circumstances surrounding the intervention of the creditor holding $2500 in bonds and attacking the validity of the statute were disclosed when he was subpoenaed and examined by counsel for the SEC. It turned out that he was a dentist who had bought the securities through a local brokerage office, and his broker had asked him to sign the document which constituted the intervening petition. The circumstances are best revealed in his testimony:

A. He simply called me up and said that there was a reorganization taking place, or they wanted to reorganize the company and wanted to know if

I would sign some papers in regard to it. That is all I know.

Q. Did he describe the papers to you?

A. No sir, he said he would bring them up.

Q. Did he tell who was going to be your lawyer?

A. I think he said something about a Mr. Davis being in town representing the company.

Q. Representing the company? A. Yes.

Q. Did he say that Mr. Davis was going to represent you?

A. No, sir.

Q. And you have never met Mr. Davis? A. No, sir.

Q. Nor Mr. Piper? A. No, sir.

Q. And where was this petition which you signed, when was it signed?

A. I judge about a week ago, a week or ten days ago. I paid no particular attention to the date.

Q. Where did you sign it?

A. Down in the attorney's office . . .

Q. Well, tell the circumstances of your signing it.

A. I asked why I was called to sign it, and after I signed it they sort of smiled and said, Well, you are the only one in Baltimore owned any of it.

Q. And did you know the contents of that petition?

A. I read it.

Q. Well, did you appreciate the contents of it?

A. As best that I could. I could not remember it now.

Q. Could you or not give your judgment as to what was in the paper that you signed?

A. Just something that they wanted to reorganize the company whereby they could realize something out of it. Otherwise, the way I understand it, the

Government was trying to confiscate the holding company or something of that kind.

Q. You don't know the circumstances of the — you don't recall the particular allegation in the petition?

A. I can not say that I do.

Q. And was it explained to you that the Government was going to confiscate the property of the utilities?

A. No, that is the way I understood it.

Q. Was any explanation given of the nature of this paper? . . .

A. No. The paper was simply brought up to me and asked me to sign it. I said, You are asking me to sign something I haven't had a chance to read, I would like to read it. I thought it was my duty to sign it, and therefore I signed the paper. According to the contents of it it sounded logical to me.

Q. Did you have an appreciation that at that time you were being represented by Mr. Davis of New York?

A. Not I, personally, no.

Q. You have never met Mr. Davis personally?

A. I don't know the gentleman.

Q. You never made any arrangements to pay any attorney any fee for representing you?

A. No, sir.

Q. You never made any arrangements to retain an attorney to act for you personally in your interest?

A. No, sir.[22]

On cross-examination, the witness agreed to be represented by the designated counsel.[23]

The district court refused to dismiss or delay the proceedings and rendered a decision declaring the entire statute unconstitutional.[24] This decision was affirmed by the circuit court of appeals.[25] Both sides, that is, the two creditors, joined in asking the Supreme Court to take the case on certiorari in order that a prompt decision could be had. At this point government counsel made a last effort to prevent this case from being the vehicle for a decision on the validity of the act. The government filed a memorandum in the Supreme Court as a friend of the court urging the inappropriateness of the case and asking that certiorari be denied. The Supreme Court denied certiorari.[26] Thus the campaign to make this the test case finally failed.

Meanwhile the government was besieged with dozens of injunction suits scattered over the country brought by utility companies to restrain the enforcement of the act prior to the date for registration. In order to hold these cases in abeyance, the government took defensive action. All government officers who might have had authority to take steps toward the enforcement of the act were instructed to do nothing pending a decision by the Supreme Court in a test case. The Postmaster General so instructed local postmasters with respect to their power over the mails; the Attorney General so instructed United States attorneys with respect to their power to commence criminal proceedings; and the SEC itself disclaimed any intention to enforce the statute until a test of the registration provisions could be had. In order to encourage the companies to register and to contest specific applications of the act later if they were so inclined, the Commission announced that registration would not waive any constitutional objections that might subsequently be raised, and that if any court should hold that registration was a waiver, the registration should be considered to be rescinded. The most serious of the injunction suits were those in the District of Columbia, where jurisdiction could be had over the members of the Commission. In these suits, the Attorney General took the unusual course of appearing in the district court and himself arguing for a stay order until a case which meanwhile was brought in the federal court in New York could be decided. The New York case was planned by the SEC as the test case; it involved Electric Bond & Share Company and was a proceeding to compel it to register, with the company filing a cross-bill asking that the act as a whole and its various control provisions in particular be declared unconstitutional. The District of Columbia court granted a stay in the cases pending before it, and, with some modification of its terms, the stay order was approved by the Supreme Court.[27] So at last the way was cleared for the test case which in due course wound its way from the district court in New York through the circuit court of appeals and to the Supreme Court, and which resulted in a decision upholding the registration provisions of the act and declining to pass on the so-called control provisions.[28]

Both here and in the TVA cases, the basic contest was over the scope of the issues. If the government could keep the case within a relatively narrow compass, it could confidently expect success. The opposition staked its chances on opening up the statutes to the widest possible attack before the government had a chance to settle down to the task of administering them. The fate of the statutes may well have turned on *how* the constitutional questions were presented.

The "how" of constitutional litigation shades off into the "when," or perhaps I should say the "whether." The timing of constitutional litigation may be of critical importance. Should the determination of constitutional issues be postponed or expedited? This raises questions of policy that affect the Court, the government, and the public. Traditionally, the Court professes never to decide a constitutional question unless and until it is necessary to the decision of an actual controversy. I have suggested that when the Court has departed from this principle, it has sometimes produced self-inflicted wounds. The fallibility of judges, and the enormously difficult task of overcoming an adverse decision through constitutional amendment, as well as the possibility of working a change in the law through the political processes, all indicate the wisdom of a policy of "sufficient unto the day is the evil thereof." This, however, requires some qualification. In the case of laws which interfere with freedom of expression or other civil and political rights, the channels of orderly change are by hypothesis clogged, and intervention by the Court at an early stage has some special justification.

From the standpoint of the government, that is, those charged with administering the laws, there can be no generalization regarding the wisdom of delay or expedition in constitutional cases, nor was there any general practice in this regard in recent years. The Gold Clause cases were expedited to the limit; in one of the cases the government petitioned for certiorari prior to argument of the case in the circuit court of appeals, and the petition was granted despite the fact that the government, seeking review, had been the successful party in the district court.[29] In the Social Security cases, the time elapsed between the bringing of the cases and the final decision in the Supreme Court was a matter only of months.[30] On the other hand, the government made no effort to secure an early decision on the NIRA, and in fact on the eve of argument in the Supreme Court dismissed a case which it had appealed and which seemed destined to be the test case.[31] And in the TVA and Holding Company litigation, as we have seen, the government was more anxious that the right case be decided than that a case be decided early.

These differences are not the result of pure caprice. They depend on a number of factors. Does the law look toward administrative case-by-case application? The Gold Clause legislation operated of its own force without implementation. This was not true of the Holding Company Act. How serious will be the uncertainty pending a decision? Uncertainty regarding the social security legislation meant uncertainty regarding a major item in the budget. It is true that uncertainty regarding the NIRA helped to undermine its administration, but it was doubtless felt that this incident of delay was outweighed by the fact that the statute could best be judged by examining its application to specific industries in specific codes, and the fact that in any event the statute was to expire two years after its enactment, and Congress was entitled to learn from its own mistakes before learning from the Supreme Court. And it would be less than candid not to add that an appraisal of the temper of the Court plays its part. And so the question whether to use Fabian tactics or push for a quick decision is a major problem of policy for government counsel. In resolving the problem, the public interest must not be overlooked. Uncertainty regarding the gold-clause legislation meant uncertainty in countless day-to-day business transactions. Uncertainty regarding the TVA and the Holding Company Act caused inconvenience to a smaller though substantial number of people; but the adverse effect of the Acts on those concerned was not so certain.

The order in which cases are brought is often of first importance. As we are reminded by Edgar in

King Lear, Ripeness is all. Or, to change the figure, it is easier to establish a proposition of law in two jumps than in one. It was easier to hold that Congress could prohibit outright the interstate shipment of goods made by child labor after the Court had held that Congress could prohibit the interstate shipment of prison-made goods into states which prohibit the local sale of such goods.[32] The fact that the Congressional policy was tied in to the local policy was a bridge that helped in crossing the constitutional gap; and when once the crossing had been made, it was possible for the Court to burn the bridge behind it. It was the policy of taking two steps instead of one that largely accounted for the government's action in dismissing in the Supreme Court the Louisville slum-clearance case, which would have tested the power of eminent domain in aid of spending for the general welfare.[33] At that time, the general welfare clause had not been authoritatively construed, and it was felt that the question of eminent domain ought to await the decision of a case involving simply the spending power without any question of compulsory taking of property. The tactics here employed resemble somewhat the military tactics which Marshal Foch is said to have urged on younger officers. He advised them to watch the movement of a parrot in its cage, which progresses by reaching out one claw, grasping firmly, and pausing before bringing the other claw into position — grasp, pause, grasp, pause, was his description of successful forward movement, and whatever its application to modern warfare, it is not a bad motto for constitutional litigation.

The opportunity which government counsel enjoy of planning and timing, within limits, the sequence of litigation, carries with it a corresponding responsibility of consistency and candor. It was decided in the mid-nineteen-thirties, with approval on the highest administrative level, to move toward an end of intergovernmental tax immunities for private taxpayers.[34] Government counsel initiated the movement by arguing as *amicus curiae* that the states have power to tax contractors on federal projects on their gross receipts including sums received from the government.[35] This was a notable piece of self-denial, since costs to the government might be increased by reason of these taxes. But the problem was a reciprocal one, and later the government was able consistently to argue for the validity of a federal tax on salaries of state employees, and still later, and consistently, as *amicus curiae* for the

validity of a state tax on salaries of federal employees.[36] But having displayed this degree of dis-
interestedness, the Department of Justice came under great pressure from budget-conscious depart-
ments to reassert the doctrine of immunity for contractors under cost-plus arrangements with the government, and when counsel yielded to the pressure
the government was rebuffed by the Court.[37] The
momentum of the government's march was not to
be stopped at its will. Mr. Justice Roberts subsequently observed pointedly that "the Government
repented its generosity." [38]

Of course there are circumstances when counsel
cannot safely abandon a position of protecting the
pecuniary interests of their client, the Federal
Treasury, until the Supreme Court speaks. On one
occasion the government was taxing certain transfers under the gift tax as completed gifts or under
the estate tax as inchoate transfers, depending on
the advantages to the Treasury in each case, pending clarification of the issue by the Supreme Court.
Companion cases reached the Court, in which the
government had taken contradictory legal positions.
They were argued in succession by the same counsel
for the government, who insisted in the one that
the transfer was a completed gift and with equal

earnestness in the other that the same kind of transfer was testamentary. This understandably perplexed counsel for the second taxpayer, who complained to the Court that the government's argument had straddled the fence. Chief Justice Hughes interposed, "I should say rather that Miss Carloss has managed to alight gracefully on both sides of the fence."

Candor has impelled counsel for the government to confess error in a substantial number of cases reaching the Supreme Court on the opponent's petition. Sometimes the government is more royalist than the King, and its exercise of a judicious temperament is met by a resistant Court, who refuse to agree that the government's case is hopeless. On one occasion a member of the Court was heard to complain that he thought "the Court is entitled to more advocacy from the Government." In the long run, candor is not simply its own reward. Mr. Justice Holmes once complimented a Solicitor General on his candor before the Court. As the Solicitor General was drawing himself up in satisfaction, Holmes added, "You know, candor is one of the most effective instruments of deception."

What can be said of the rôle of counsel in constitutional litigation in the future? Government counsel will, of course, retain in delicate balance their threefold responsibility — to the Court, to the administrative agencies, and to the public. Counsel for both government and private interests will do well to heed the lesson that the reach must not exceed the grasp. Declaratory judgments and broad injunctions are tempting, but those seeking them are frequently left empty-handed. It is sounder to argue a constitutional case as a case, arguing for victory on constitutional grounds if need be, but above all arguing the case and not an abstract question of constitutional law. This does not mean that constitutional questions should be ignored in the early stages of the case. On the contrary, counsel may find that, unless they have raised the questions at an early stage, so that the lower court is called on to consider them, the Supreme Court will refuse to pass on them. Constitutional questions should be envisaged at the earliest possible stage in the litigation, and should be appropriately raised by pleadings and evidence; but they should not be developed to the exclusion of other issues on which the case may be decided.

The Supreme Court's recent reluctance to declare state laws unconstitutional under the due-process clause unless basic civil liberties are involved has important implications for litigation. The result may well be that constitutional litigation over state laws will be concentrated more and more in state courts under state constitutional provisions, and state constitutional law may become of dominant importance. In the field of federal legislation, the constitutional issues may be increasingly diverted from the federal courts to the legislative stage, so that the constitutional lawyer's function will be discharged more frequently before Congressional committees than in court. Constitutional law may thus become one phase of legislative drafting. This centering of constitutional debate is salutary, subject to two cautions: The constitutional validity of a bill must not be taken to resolve questions of its wisdom, and *per contra*, some constitutional doubts about a bill need not debar its passage. The legislature has to reach a final collective judgment on the merits of proposed legislation; it does not have to pass finally on constitutionality.

And so in finding a rôle for "Judge and Company" in constitutional law, we are led back to our starting point, to the place of the Court in the complex of government. We have arrived full circle at the problem of the One and the Many.

Notes

INTRODUCTION

[1] Fairman, *Mr. Justice Miller and the Supreme Court* (Cambridge: Harvard University Press, 1939), 232.

I. CONCORD AND DISCORD

[1] Whitehead, *Essays in Science and Philosophy* (1947), 130.

[2] Address of Chief Justice Hughes, 13 Proc. Am. L. Inst. 61, 64 (1936): "How amazing it is that, in the midst of controversies on every conceivable subject, one should expect unanimity of opinion upon difficult legal questions! In the highest ranges of thought, in theology, philosophy and science, we find differences of view on the part of the most distinguished experts, — theologians, philosophers and scientists. The history of scholarship is a record of disagreements. And when we deal with questions relating to principles of law and their application, we do not suddenly rise into a stratosphere of icy certainty."

[3] West Virginia State Board of Education v. Barnette, 319 U.S. 624 (1943). The earlier cases are Leoles v. Lander, 302 U.S. 656 (1937); Hering v. State Board of Education, 303 U.S. 624 (1938).

[4] Grovey v. Townsend, 295 U.S. 45 (1935); Smith v. Allwright, 321 U.S. 649 (1944).

[5] Shelley v. Kramer, 334 U.S. 1 (1948). The earlier case is Corrigan v. Buckley, 271 U.S. 323 (1926).

[6] Commonwealth v. Davis, 162 Mass. 510, 511 (1895). Cf. Hague v. CIO, 307 U.S. 496 (1939).

[7] United Public Workers v. Mitchell, 330 U.S. 75 (1947), quoting (at p. 99, n. 34) Holmes's remark in McAuliffe v. New Bedford, 155 Mass. 216, 220 (1891).

[8] Kovacs v. Cooper, 336 U.S. 77, 95 (1949) (concurring).

[9] Cf. Hocking, *Freedom of the Press* (Chicago: University of Chicago Press, 1947), 60–61: "The right of freedom is based on the value of freedom but is not identical with that value. . . . Why is one not free to abandon his freedom; why may he not sell himself into slavery? Because, quite apart from his inclination, he has a duty to live as a man and assume the burden of self-guidance. He owes this to his own dignity; he owes it also to the common concern that human dignity shall be upheld." *Id.* at 96–97: "If a man is burdened with an idea, he not only desires to express it; he ought to express it. . . . It is the duty of the scientist or the discoverer to his result, of Confucius to his teaching, of Socrates to his oracle. It is the duty of every man to his belief. It is not limited to special persons and special occasions; it has a certain totality. . . . In any case, one's relation to what he himself *sees* constitutes for him a major obligation, and the freedom of expression here merges with freedom of conscience."

[10] Cf. the well-known statement of Stone, J., in United States v. Carolene Products Co., 304 U.S. 144, 152, n. 4 (1938):

It is unnecessary to consider now whether legislation which restricts those political processes which can ordinarily be expected to bring about repeal of undesirable legislation, is to be subjected to more exacting judicial scrutiny under the general prohibitions of the Fourteenth Amendment than are most other types of legislation. . . .

Nor need we enquire whether similar considerations enter into the review of statutes directed at particular religious . . . or national . . . or racial minorities . . .: whether prejudice against discrete and insular minorities may be a special condition, which tends seriously to curtail the operation of those political processes ordinarily to be relied upon to protect minorities, and which may call for a correspondingly more searching judicial inquiry. Compare McCulloch v. Maryland, 4 Wheat, 316, 428; South Carolina v. Barnwell Bros., 303 U.S. 177, 184, n. 2, and cases cited.

When we move from legislative clogs on the political processes themselves, in the large sense, to the kind of legislation dealt with at the end of the final paragraph, there is the difficulty of distinguishing between minorities of the kind specified and some economic minority interests, so far as concerns the operation of representative government through majority rule. The cases last cited in the paragraph are distinctive, since they are instances of local economic interests working against the outsider, raising problems of federalism.

[11] See Charles Warren, "The New 'Liberty' under the Fourteenth Amendment," 39 Harv. L. Rev. 431 (1926).

[12] L. Hand, "Chief Justice Stone's Conception of the Judicial Function," 46 Col. L. Rev. 696, 698 (1946).

[13] *Discourses on Davila* (1789–1790), quoted in Coker, *Democracy, Liberty, and Property* (New York: The Macmillan Co., 1947), 466.

[14] "A Defence of the Constitutions of Government of the United States of America," in J. Adams, *Works* (C. F. Adams, ed., 1851), vol. VI, p. 9.

[15] *Construction Construed, and Constitutions Vindicated* (1820), quoted in Coker, *op. cit., supra,* note 13, at 495–496.

[16] Journal of Debates and Proceedings in the Convention of Delegates Chosen to Revise the Constitution of Massachusetts, 1820 (1853), 312.

[17] Letter to Moss Kent, in *Memoirs and Letters of James Kent* (1898), 218.

[18] *The Law of Love and Love as Law* (1868), 182–183, quoted in Gabriel, *The Course of American Democratic Thought* (New York: The Ronald Press, 1940), 149.

[19] *Shelburne Essays*, 9th series (Boston: Houghton Mifflin Co., 1915), 136 (italics in original). For the reference I am indebted to Professor Merle Curti of the University of Wisconsin. Cf. also Babbitt, *Democracy and Leadership* (1924), 307–308.

[20] Lincoln Federal Labor Union v. Northwestern Iron & Metal Co., 335 U.S. 525 (1949).

[21] *Freedom of the Press, op. cit., supra*, note 9, at 56.

[22] Reprinted in Wolfe, *Leveller Manifestoes of the Puritan Revolution* (New York: Thos. Nelson & Sons, 1944), 400, 409.

[23] Reprinted in Edman, *Fountainheads of Freedom* (New York: Harcourt, Brace & Co., 1941), 320, 324–325.

[24] Murdock v. Pennsylvania, 319 U.S. 105 (1943) (Roberts, Reed, Frankfurter, and Jackson, JJ., dissenting); Martin v. Struthers, 319 U.S. 141 (1943) (Roberts, Reed, Frankfurter, and Jackson, JJ., dissenting; Douglas, Murphy, and Rutledge, JJ., concurring specially); Saia v. New York, 334 U.S. 558 (1948) (Reed, Frankfurter, Jackson, and Burton, JJ., dissenting); cf. Kovacs v. Cooper, *supra*, note 8 (Black, Douglas, Murphy, and Rutledge, JJ., dissenting; Frankfurter and Jackson, JJ., concurring specially).

[25] In re Summers, 325 U.S. 561 (1945) (Black, Douglas, Murphy, and Rutledge, JJ., dissenting).

[26] Harris v. United States, 331 U.S. 145 (1947) (upholding seizure, without a search warrant, of unlawfully possessed draft cards after intensive search of premises pursuant to warrant of arrest for unrelated offense; Frankfurter, Murphy, Jackson, and Rutledge, JJ., dissenting); Johnson v. United States, 333 U.S. 10 (1948) (invalidating search and seizure of opium and smoking apparatus in living quarters, without warrant of arrest or of search; Vinson, C.J., Black, Reed, and Burton, JJ., dissenting); Trupiano v. United States, 334 U.S. 699 (1948) (invalidating seizure of contraband property, where arrest was lawful but no search warrant was obtained and failure not justified by emergency; Vinson, C.J., Black, Reed, and Burton, JJ., dissenting).

[27] Commonwealth v. Peaslee, 177 Mass. 267, 272 (1901); cf. also Swift & Co. v. United States, 196 U.S. 375, 396 (1905); Hyde v. United States, 225 U.S. 347, 387–388 (1912) (dissenting).

[28] Bridges v. California, 314 U.S. 252 (1941) (Stone, C.J., Roberts, Frankfurter, and Byrnes, JJ., dissenting).

[29] United Public Workers v. Mitchell, *supra,* note 7 (Black, Douglas, and Rutledge, JJ., dissenting; Frankfurter, J., concurring specially; Murphy and Jackson, JJ., not participating).

[30] McNabb v. United States, 318 U.S. 332 (1943).

[31] Townsend v. Burke, 334 U.S. 736, 738 (1948).

[32] Fisher v. United States, 328 U.S. 463 (1946).

[33] Uveges v. Pennsylvania, 335 U.S. 437, 449–450 (1948) (dissenting).

[34] Pinkerton v. United States, 328 U.S. 640 (1946); Kotteakos v. United States, 328 U.S. 750 (1946); see Krulewitch v. United States, 336 U.S. 440 (1949).

[35] Adamson v. California, 332 U.S. 46, 68–123 (1947) (dissenting).

[36] *Id.* at 69–70, 77–78, 90, 91. See also the concurring opinion in International Shoe Co. v. Washington, 326 U.S. 310, 322 (1945).

[37] Connecticut Gen. Life Ins. Co. v. Johnson, 303 U.S. 77, 83 (1938) (dissenting).

[38] 307 U.S. 496, 500 (1939).

[39] 314 U.S. at 280.

[40] 332 U.S. at 71.

[41] Frank, Book Review, 24 Ind. L. J. 139, 144, n. 10 (1948).

[42] "Science and Morals" (1886), in *Evolution and Ethics, and Other Essays* (1897), 128.

[43] Johnson v. Zerbst, 304 U.S. 458 (1938).

[44] Betts v. Brady, 316 U.S. 455 (1942); Bute v. Illinois, 333 U.S. 640 (1948). The thesis that the workings of Federalism would be promoted, not exacerbated, by enforcing the right to counsel against the states in all criminal cases is ably presented in J. R. Green, "The Bill of Rights, the Fourteenth Amendment and the Supreme Court," 46 Mich. L. Rev. 869 (1948).

[45] H. A. L. Fisher, *Maitland* (1910), 67.

[46] United States v. South-Eastern Underwriters Assn., 322 U.S. 533 (1944) (departing from precedent; Stone, C.J., Frankfurter and Jackson, JJ., dissenting; Roberts and Reed, JJ., not participating).

[47] Helvering v. Griffiths, 318 U.S. 371 (1943) (adhering to precedent; Douglas, Black, and Murphy, JJ., dissenting; Rutledge, J., not participating).

[48] Girouard v. United States, 328 U.S. 61 (1946) (departing from precedent; Stone, C.J., Reed and Frankfurter, JJ., dissenting; Jackson, J., not participating).

[49] Cleveland v. United States, 329 U.S. 14 (1946) (adhering to precedent; Black, Murphy, and Jackson, JJ., dissenting; Rutledge, J., concurring specially).

[50] 318 U.S. at 408.

[51] Helvering v. Griffiths, *supra*, note 47, at 403–404; United States v. California, 332 U.S. 19, 45–46 (1947) (dissent); Commissioner v. Estate of Church, 335 U.S. 632, 685, n. 14 (1949) (dissent).

[52] Helvering v. Gerhardt, 304 U.S. 405 (1938).

[53] Message from the President, April 25, 1938, 83 Cong. Rec. 5683.

[54] Memorandum in Reply to Petition for Rehearing in Helvering v. Gerhardt (*supra*, note 52), at 16–18.

[55] 53 Stat. 575.

[56] L. Hand, "Thomas Walter Swan," 57 Yale L. J. 167, 172 (1947).

II. PORTRAIT OF A LIBERAL JUDGE

[1] Pollock v. Farmers' Loan & Trust Co., 158 U.S. 601, 695 (1895).

[2] Liverpool, New York & Philadelphia SS. Co. v. Commissioners of Emigration, 113 U.S. 33, 39 (1885).

[3] Chicago, M. & St. P. Ry. v. Minnesota, 134 U.S. 418 (1890) (dissent); Wabash, St. L. & P. Ry. v. Illinois, 118 U.S. 557 (1886) (dissent). See Fairman, "The Education of a Justice," 1 Stanford L. Rev. 217, 218–219 (1949). Compare Bradley's earlier views in Davidson v. New Orleans, 96 U.S. 97, 107 (1878).

[4] Introduction to "The Sins of Legislators," in Spencer, *The Man Versus the State* (Caldwell, Idaho: The Caxton Printers, Ltd., Truxton Beale, ed., 1916. Used by special permission of the copyright owners.), 241.

[5] Brandeis, "The Employer and Trades Unions" (1904), and "Organized Labor and Efficiency" (1911), printed in *Business — A Profession* (1933 ed.), 13, 37.

[6] "Knowledge is essential to understanding; and understanding should precede judging." Jay Burns Baking Co. v. Bryan, 264 U.S. 504, 520 (1924) (dissenting).

[7] Nashville, C. & St. L. Ry. v. Walters, 294 U.S. 405 (1935). Cf. also Hammond v. Schappi Bus Line, 275 U.S. 164 (1927).

[8] Carmichael v. Southern Coal Co., 301 U.S. 495 (1937).

[9] Texas & Pacific Ry. v. Pottorff, 291 U.S. 245 (1934); McNair v. Knott, 302 U.S. 369 (1937). Cf. also Lewis v. Fidelity & Deposit Co. of Maryland, 292 U.S. 559 (1934).

[10] New State Ice Co. v. Liebmann, 285 U.S. 262, 309–311 (1932) (dissenting).

[11] Liggett v. Lee, 288 U.S. 517, 541 (1933) (dissenting).

[12] Ashwander v. TVA, 297 U.S. 288, 341 (1936) (concurring).

[13] 304 U.S. 64 (1938).

[14] Willing v. Chicago Auditorium Assn., 277 U.S. 274 (1928); Nashville, C. & St. L. Ry. v. Wallace, 288 U.S. 249 (1933).

[15] Northern Pac. Ry. v. Department of Public Works, 268 U.S. 39, 44–45 (1925).

[16] Oklahoma Operating Co. v. Love, 252 U.S. 331, 338 (1920).

[17] St. Joseph Stock Yards Co. v. United States, 298 U.S. 38, 77 (1936) (concurring).

[18] Whitney v. California, 274 U.S. 357, 372 (1927) (concurring).

[19] Senn v. Tile Layers Protective Union, 301 U.S. 468, 478 (1937).

[20] Duplex Printing Press Co. v. Deering, 254 U.S. 443, 488 (1921) (dissenting).

[21] 248 U.S. 215, 248 (1918) (dissenting).

[22] 262 U.S. 553, 605 (1923) (dissenting).

[23] Dahnke-Walker Milling Co. v. Bondurant, 257 U.S. 282, 293 (1921) (dissenting).

[24] *Dissertationes,* Bk. III, ch. 24, quoted in 6 Toynbee, *A Study of History,* 147, n. 1 (1939). For a penetrating treatment of Stoicism and advocacy, see Curtis, "A Lawyer's 'Entire' Devotion to his Client," 34 A. B. A. J. 805 (1948).

[25] Bradford Electric Light Co. v. Clapper, 284 U.S. 221 (1931).

[26] John Hancock Mutual Life Ins. Co. v. Yates, 299 U.S. 178 (1936).

[27] Yarborough v. Yarborough, 290 U.S. 202 (1933).

[28] Hearings before Committee on the Judiciary, U. S. Senate, 74th Cong. 1st sess., on S. 2176, p. 10.

[29] 254 U.S. 325 (1920).

[30] 262 U.S. 390 (1923).

[31] Casey v. United States, 276 U.S. 413 (1928).

[32] 271 U.S. 142 (1926).

[33] Burnet v. Coronado Oil & Gas Co., 285 U.S. 393, 406 (1932) (dissenting).

[34] *Supra,* note 13.

[35] Conversely, his approach to the problem of education reflected his attachment to Federalism; witness his selection of the University of Louisville as an object of his bounty and solicitude. Bernard Flexner's monograph, *Mr. Justice Brandeis and the University of Louisville* (1938) gives a most revealing insight into Brandeis's insistence on both vision and mastery of detail, in the context of an endeavor to enrich the life of a state.

III. "JUDGE AND COMPANY" IN CONSTITUTIONAL LAW

[1] *Theaetetus* (Jowett translation).

[2] "Augustus Noble Hand," 61 Harv. L. Rev. 573, 585.

[3] 316 U.S. 455 (1942).

[4] Korematsu v. United States, 323 U.S. 214 (1944).

[5] 1 Warren, *Supreme Court in United States History* (rev. ed., 1937), 610–611.

[6] 7 How. 1 (1849).

[7] 11 *Writings and Speeches of Daniel Webster* (Boston: Little, Brown & Co., 1903), 219.

[8] Norman v. Baltimore & Ohio RR., 294 U.S. 240 (1935).

[9] Hughes, *The Supreme Court of the United States* (1928), 50–54.

[10] Cf. Norman v. Consolidated Edison Co., 89 F. (2d) 619 (C. A. 2d, 1937).

[11] E.g., Moor v. Texas & N. O. R. Co., 297 U.S. 101 (1936).

[12] Muller v. Oregon, 208 U.S. 412 (1908). The opinion of the Court, upholding the law, was delivered by Mr. Justice Brewer, generally not distinguished for sympathy toward social legislation. He did, however, exhibit marked sympathy for womankind; see, e.g., In re Bort, 25 Kans. 308 (1881). He stands as a reminder that sentimentality in a judge is not an adequate substitute for a philosophy of government.

[13] Argument in Stettler v. O'Hara, 243 U.S. 629 (1917), printed in *The Curse of Bigness: Miscellaneous Papers of Justice Brandeis* (New York: The Viking Press, Fraenkel, ed., 1934), 52, 65–66.

[14] Carter v. Carter Coal Co., 298 U.S. 238 (1936).

[15] Alabama Power Co. v. Ickes, 302 U.S. 464 (1938).

[16] Tennessee Electric Power Co. v. TVA, 306 U.S. 118 (1939).

[17] Ashwander v. TVA, 297 U.S. 288 (1936).

[18] 90 F. (2d) 885 (C. A. 6th, 1937).

[19] *Supra*, note 16.

[20] In re American States Public Service Co., 12 F. Supp. 667 (D. Md., 1935).

[21] In re Central West Public Service Co., 13 F. Supp. 239 (D. Del., 1935).

[22] Transcript of Record, pp. 304–305, in Burco v. Whitworth, reported at 81 F. (2d) 721 (C. A. 4th, 1936).

[23] *Id.* at 306.

[24] *Supra,* note 20.

[25] Burco v. Whitworth, *supra*, note 22.

[26] Burco v. Whitworth, 297 U.S. 724 (1936).

[27] Landis v. North American Co., 299 U.S. 248 (1936).

[28] Electric Bond & Share Co. v. SEC, 303 U.S. 419 (1938).

[29] United States v. Bankers Trust Co., 294 U.S. 240 (1935).

[30] Helvering v. Davis, 301 U.S. 619 (1937). The decision of the district court was rendered on January 27, 1937; that of the Circuit Court of Appeals on April 14; and that of the Supreme Court on May 24.

[31] United States v. Belcher, 294 U.S. 736 (1935).

[32] United States v. Darby, 312 U.S. 100 (1941); Kentucky Whip & Collar Co. v. Illinois Central RR., 299 U.S. 334 (1937).

[33] United States v. Certain Lands in Louisville, 297 U.S. 726 (1936).

[34] See page 41, *supra.*

[35] James v. Dravo Contracting Co., 302 U.S. 134 (1937).

[36] Helvering v. Gerhardt, 304 U.S. 405 (1938) (in which

the Court's decision was more sweeping than the government's argument; see page 41, *supra*); Graves v. New York ex rel. O'Keefe, 306 U.S. 466 (1939).

[37] Alabama v. King & Boozer, 314 U.S. 1 (1941).

[38] United States v. Allegheny County, 322 U.S. 174, 193 (1944) (dissenting).

Index